# kill

## Sue Arrington

# Acknowledgements

## Killin' Snakes painting by: Jon Fuchs

## Edited by: Dr. Cara Snyder

THE HOLY BIBLE, NEW INTERNATIONAL VERSION®, NIV® Copyright © 1973, 1978, 1984, 2011 by Biblica, Inc.® Used by permission. All rights reserved worldwide.

Scripture taken from the NEW AMERICAN STANDARD BIBLE®, Copyright © 1960,1962,1963,1968,1971,1972,1973,1975,1977,1995 by The Lockman Foundation. Used by permission.

Scripture quotations marked "KJV" are taken from the Holy Bible, King James Version, Cambridge, 1769.

Scripture quotations marked "NRSV" are taken from the Holy Bible, *New Revised Standard Version of the Bible* published, National Council of Churches, 1989

Symptoms of Demonic Operation- Article by Ron Phillips, Charisma Magazine

Snake Charming – Wikipedia

The Spirit of Python – Prophetic Insight, Christy Johnson, Charisma Magazine, 4/25/2017

Venomous Snakes-Wikipedia

103 Breaking the Power of Leviathan – Truth and Freedom Ministries

Susannah (Book of Daniel)- Wikipedia

Cover graphics adapted from digital artwork-Freepix.com

ISBN-13:978-1721772681
ISBN-10:1721772685

# Endorsements

*Killin Snakes, is a powerful account of God's faithfulness and His redeeming work so personally expressed in the pain of life. Sue Arrington with raw honesty shares her pain and the wonder of God's grace. This is a personal and compelling testimony that will bless and encourage every reader. I could not put it down!*
    **Tom Lane, Lead Executive Apostolic Pastor, Gateway Church**

*"If the art of living is the ability to use hardships in a constructive fashion, Sue Arrington has provided a superb example of how this is to be accomplished . . . Killin' Snakes sizzles with vulnerable mistakes and brave comebacks we all should learn from. A Brilliant piece of work!"*
**Liz Morris, The Personality Doctor and Best-Selling Author of Seekers, A World Within a World and Founder of The Dallas Dream Team."**

*Killin' Snakes is a compelling story of God's ability to redeem each of us. Regardless of the mistakes you may have made in your own life, Killin' Snakes will inspire you to believe God to "cause all things to work together for good." The author writes with a captivating narrative style that will engage your attention from the first page to the last. If you need God to redeem your life, I commend Killin' Snakes to you.*
    **Mike Downey, President, Strategic Impact**

*The battle between good and evil is real and Sue's story illustrates the importance of recognizing the ways of our enemy. Her gripping account of her miraculous transformation shares her rescue and devotion to her hero, God. The reader will come face to face with all the emotions, trials, failures and successes Sue experienced on this incredible journey. Her deliverer's victory, will inspire, inform, and challenges her readers. A must-read!*
    **Donna Skell, Executive Director of Roaring Lambs Ministries**

This book is dedicated to Kent; my husband, my best friend, and my partner in ministry. You like to quote your father Dee's words, which you have labeled as, "Dee-ism's". The one you quote the most is also my favorite and I believe to be the thread running through our relationship, "It is not always easy to love but it is always necessary." You have shown such great love to me especially when I was not easy to love. Thank you for not only listening to your earthly father but always seeking the direction of your Heavenly Father. I love you "Phat Daddy."

# Table of Contents

**Chapter 1**
The Serpent.................................................................. Page 9

**Chapter 2**
Killin' Snakes................................................................Page 19

**Chapter 3**
The Charming Serpent ...............................................Page 30

**Chapter 4**
The Fiery Serpent........................................................Page 37

**Chapter 5**
The Fleeing Serpent ...................................................Page 51

**Chapter 6**
The Snake Path ...........................................................Page 68

**Chapter 7**
Snake Hunter...............................................................Page 84

**Chapter 8**
The Venomous Serpent...............................................Page 93

**Chapter 9**
The Snake Pit Revisited ............................................Page 123

**Chapter 10**
The Raised Serpent ...................................................Page 169

**Chapter 11**
Jesus the Antivenom.................................................Page 193

# PREFACE

WHILE ON A recent trip to Israel, I was able to visualize the ancient tribes wandering in the desert, having fled captivity in Egypt, only to come to a place where they did not care to be and complaining to God, even blaming him for their predicament. For most of my life, it seemed to me that I too was wandering in the desert, fleeing from one bad situation to another and at one point raising my fist to heaven, crying out at God in anger, also blaming Him for my circumstances.

There, in Israel, while standing overlooking the valley of Megiddo, I became enthralled by our tour guide's detailed description of the excavation site and the towering stone walls before us which composed layer upon layer of civilizations separated by rough-hewn horizontal wooden beams, a sort of Dagwood sandwich of biblical history. Walking amid the ruins provided a respite from the sweltering heat, and as I moved closer to one of the towering walls, seeking shade, my attention was drawn to a crevice in the wall immediately to my left. There, just above me, was a black snakelike creature crawling between the ancient stones. Immediately these words were dropped into my spirit, "This is the beginning of your story, the one you have been seeking all these years."

In reality the serpentine creature in the crevice was not a snake but a ten-inch-long millipede, a relative of a creature thought to have inhabited the earth millions of years ago. As it crept its way in and out of the stone foundations of these ancient cities, I realized that Satan the snake, in his various forms, has been slithering in and out of the lives of civilizations for centuries from the beginning, just as he has been slipping in and out of my life and the lives of my family members for generations. Then these words echoed through my soul: One day the very stones of these ancient assembled walls which now testify to ages past will stand as silent sentinels high above the battlefield below where the snake Satan will meet his destruction, the ultimate battle for the power and control over the inhabitants of the earth, the power over our minds and bodies. Here at this place, these very stones were crying out proclaiming God's final victory over the dark prince of the earth, the serpent Satan.

I have been working on this book for the past five years. I have written probably ten different beginnings to my story. It was not until there, in Israel, standing on the hill overlooking the valley of Armageddon, the site depicted in the book of Revelation as the backdrop for the final battle between God and Satan, that God revealed to me the words I am now writing. It is with great care and at times enormous pain that I am beginning to expose the light to my own life-and-death battle with Satan and his efforts to exert his power and control over my life. It has been a battle which has caused me to explore not only a number of states and continents, but more importantly, the territories of my heart, mind, and soul, searching for the answer to the emptiness inside of me.

# CHAPTER I

## THE SERPENT

Genesis 3:1 NIV

> Now the serpent was more crafty than any of the wild animals the Lord God had made. He said to the woman, "Did God really say, 'You must not eat from any tree in the garden'?"

I HAVE READ many theories about why the serpent spoke to Eve, the woman in the Garden of Eden, first. Was it because she had such great powers of persuasion and Satan knew that if he could win her over then she would certainly be able to persuade Adam the man to follow her in this, her defiant sin? Was it because the serpent felt that Eve was weaker than Adam? Was it because, she, being a woman, was more susceptible to being enticed by beauty? I am not sure. I only know that Satan the serpent spoke to me, I listened, and I followed his leading.

Since I was given the beginning of this book while standing at Armageddon, it seems appropriate to begin this story at my personal Armageddon, May 15, 2009.

I was fifty-seven and in the recovery room of a hospital in a neighboring town only fifteen miles away from home. It was not my usual hospital, but this is the facility preferred by my doctor. I had just been through surgery to replace a broken catheter that was implanted between two vertebrae in my spine. The catheter was connected to tubing which extended from that point under the skin on my left side and attached to a pain pump implanted in my abdomen. This device had been delivering two very strong pain medications, Baclofen and morphine, into my spinal cord for the past two years.

On this particular night following my surgery I was accidentally injected with a lethal dose of morphine. The amount administered was the maximum total dosage for the next twenty-four hours, which was only to be administered in small increments and then only as needed for severe pain. Instead, I received what medical guidelines say should have been a fatal dose.

I immediately crashed into a death spiral; as they say, I coded, not once but twice. No one, absolutely no one—not I, not the person who administered the overdose, not the doctor who was frantically trying to save my life—had any inkling that this potentially fatal human error would be the catalyst for the miracle that would physically and spiritually save my life. The snake Satan, the enemy of us all, had summoned all of his forces in a dramatic attempt to put an end to me, but God was not done with me yet. Instead of ending my life, this event, this mistake, brought me to the brink of death and then into a new life.

The doctors and nurses were able to resuscitate me and I was stable for one hour whereupon I crashed a second time requiring another frantic and thank God, successful procedure to revive me. For the next 30 or so hours, I lay on life support, still and silent, on the outside. On the inside, I was engaged in a terrifying battle—the battle for my soul.

During my first encounter with death, I saw no white light, no relatives who have gone on to be with Jesus, no tunnel. What I did experience was myself looking down over the past twenty-one years of my life.

What happened next I can only describe to you as like a movie, complete with sound and color, a chronological review of the times across the previous twenty-one years of my life.

During the first episode as I lay there, somewhere between this world and the next, watching the diorama of my life unfold, I very clearly and distinctly heard God ask me,

"Do you remember this?"

Before me, I saw a time when I wasn't where I should have been.

"Yes," I replied.

And another embarrassing scene was presented to me, and once again He asked,

"Do you remember this?"

This time it was a scene where I wasn't with whom I should have been.

"Yes," I replied.

A woodpile scene appeared, a time when I was ugly to someone I loved.

He spoke, and I responded in an ever-diminishing tiny voice, "Yes."

I was ashamed, as scene after scene replayed before me—times when I had made a career and worldly things my priority instead of God, many times when I should have been a good Christian woman, wife, and mother but wasn't, times I had searched for fulfillment in things and people of this earth instead of those things of His design, times I had not asked God to forgive me, times I had let Satan the snake entwine himself into my life and hold me in his powerful grip.

Scene after scene unfolded, relationship after relationship—so many images, so much shame. I had danced with the devil on far too many occasions. It all came flooding back to me, scenes of my hidden past.

In 1998 when I was forty-six and my husband Kent and I began dating, I was still living under the belief that my past was not important to my future. I had not told him of my many indiscretions even though he had asked me about my life before him. I had only given him the Cliff's Notes version, edited to present me in the best light. I had, in reality, been led into believing that it was none of his business. The world is good at telling women that they can do it all and have it all. The magazines display picture after picture of how they perceive our life should be. If you want that career, it's yours, no matter the cost. If you want that man, you can have him; no need to marry before having sex. It's all OK.

But it isn't OK. None of it is OK. It is not OK because you cause pain to other people by living that lifestyle, you cause great pain to yourself by living that way, and most of all you cause great pain to your Father God.

What began to play before me during this flash of memory was too shameful, too dark, to excruciatingly horrible for me to think about. I saw myself and the man I had lived with outside the bonds of marriage for four torturous years. With disgust, I looked into the time in my life when I had abandoned all that I knew to be right and plunged myself into an accursed union, the very antithesis of what a good and true woman of God should do. No, I did not want to remember the next scene: this time in my life was not of someone else's design but a maze of sin and despair which I had willingly descended into. The scenes below me were all twisted and dark, scenes of me doing and saying horrible things, a time void of light. I had willfully run away into a relationship filled with vice and destruction. This was the time in my life when Satan had twisted his serpentine body around me and played a sordid tune that I had danced to. I had lived on the fifty-fourth floor of a luxury tower, but my life had descended to a basement of despair.

I remember wishing that I wanted to press the Stop button, but it seemed to be stuck in Play. These scenes my husband, the man who had so tenderly cared for me, had no knowledge of. He knew of the fact of my living arrangements, but the sordid details I had kept a dark secret. I had bought into the lies of the world which said that your past was your business; no need to confess. Scene after scene flashed before me for what seemed like an eternity but in reality could have only been a few minutes.

As I hovered somewhere between life and death, I don't remember the exact number of times that God repeated, "Remember this?" but what I do remember is that with each exchange, my voice became smaller and smaller until the great shame of all of my transgressions that had played out below me in living color had reduced my voice to only a whisper, then no voice at all.

Time had no meaning during this encounter with my history. I only have a sense that the movie ended. I felt a sensation as if a metal bullet was being injected into my arm, and I could feel it as it coursed through my body, and I was revived.

Satan was not so ready to back down from the fight. Again I coded, all signs of life fading from my body. My lung collapsed. Once again Satan the python was encircling my chest, trying to squeeze the very life out of me. I was intubated, a machine breathing for me.

Once again I envisioned a silver bullet entering my body. To this day I vividly remember that sensation and how the silver bullets felt. Upon my recovery, I recounted this story to my husband. It was then that he told me that it was necessary for the doctor to administer intravenously a potent medication, possibly Narcan, that is designed to extract all drugs from your system and is commonly used for overdose victims. The medication had cleansed my blood of the lethal drug, but at the same time, God was working, cleansing my soul of the venom of the snake. I had this serene sense of calm. I somehow knew that I had been forgiven of all of the transgressions I had kept hidden.

    It is funny, but as I envision myself lying there fighting for my life, my mind travels back to scenes from the movie *The Werewolf* and how it ultimately took a silver bullet to kill the beast. That's how I felt at that moment, as if an actual bullet of silver were coursing through my veins. I could picture the shiny orb as it entered my veins, traveling first down my left arm, then back up finding its way to my heart and then launching from there down my left side the length of my leg and back up, then the right leg, up and down along my right side, where it made a detour to my other arm, repeating its two-way journey up and down, flowing then through my neck, circling my brain and then descending again to my heart. It was not a silver bullet from a vampire-killing pistol that had entered my body. It was not just the silver needles bearing a lifesaving drug that was injected into my veins to cleanse my blood of the poison morphine that was at work. It was the power of God and the Holy Spirit alive in me working against the weakening forces of the serpent that was coursing through my veins.

    Then, the voice. This time God did not call me to witness scenes from my past. This time I heard only the sound of His tender voice calling me,

  "Get back down there. We are not done cleaning up this earth!"

    For hours I lay in a coma. On the outside were the tubes, the wires, and the machines monitoring every bodily function to detect even the slightest signs I was winning the war to regain my physical self. On the inside, I was engaged in the terrifying battle of my life.

I saw what seemed to me like hell, a very real three-dimensional hell. Every monstrous atrocity of sexual perversion I had witnessed on television and in movies, every detail of the crimes committed against the many victims I had tried to rescue at the Crisis Center where I had served as director were heaped upon the back of the personal sins I committed in my own life. This cacophony of evil took the shape of a gigantic monster which could only be compared to a beast of hell; it began to assault me relentlessly. I was chained to a platform which resembled a boxing ring but looked somewhat like the bed I slept in at home. The monster would appear from nowhere and attack. When he was finished, he would retreat into the darkness, whereupon I was compelled to clean up the carnage. Then I would wait for the next round.

It seemed to go on for an eternity. Just as I had been battling the forces of evil in the arena of this world, I was given a frighteningly clear vision of what I was designed to do: clean up the mess from Satan's attacks.

At times I heard my pain doctor's nurse say "Come back, Carol (my first name)." "Wake up Carol." "Don't go, Carol." I could clearly hear other conversations. I wanted to respond, but I couldn't. I wanted to wake up, but I couldn't. It was a living-but-not-living hell.

The nurses made comments about how good looking my husband is and how they wouldn't mind taking a shot at him—after all, this old thing had had a go at him. (My husband was forty-eight; I looked like his mother.) It made me furious. It made me want to fight to wake up, fight to live.

Again I was presented with a vision. This time there was no monster, no attack. This time I clearly saw myself in Africa standing next to a young man I thought was my younger brother. His right hand was clutching the neck of a guitar.

Up to this time, I had never thought of traveling to Africa. However, as a small child, I had accompanied my grandmother "Ma" (as she liked to be called) to church for a reception honoring a deaconess missionary visiting from China. I was fascinated by the slideshow of this young woman's journeys to a mysterious country. I remember thinking that one day I would go somewhere for God, but not China. Through over thirty moves in my life, I had managed to hold onto the two tiny cloth dolls dressed in traditional red and blue outfits that Ma purchased for me that day. I knew I would go somewhere for God.

Now, in this limbo existence where I found myself, He was showing me where? Africa. I remember having some vague knowledge that God also desired for me to be involved in a women's ministry of some kind. There were no details, no visions, only a surreal sense of knowing.

All of these visions and sensations were swirling around me in the darkness of a coma.

The medical personnel around me did not know me. I had never been a patient in the ICU of that hospital before. They did not know who I was or what shape I had been in for the previous six years. They had not seen the braces on my legs that allowed my once-active legs to walk. They only saw the evidence of what the attack of Satan had done to my body—the scar from the feeding tube, the two-hundred pounds of weight I carried, the bulging pain pump protruding from my abdomen. All they knew was that I had suffered the effects of an overdose of morphine. They only knew what they saw before them, the monitors and contraptions all providing feedback about my physical condition, none of which provided the slightest information about the battle against the powers of darkness which was going on inside the stillness of the coma.

Ephesians 6:12 NIV, says: "For we wrestle not against flesh and blood, but against principalities, against powers, against the rulers of the darkness of this world, against spiritual wickedness in high places."

The people surrounding me could not have known how or why I had arrived there that day in their particular recovery room. Only God knew the reason.

# CHAPTER 2

## KILLIN' SNAKES

Luke 10:19 NIV

I have given you authority to trample on snakes and scorpions and to overcome all the power of the enemy; nothing will harm you

MY LIFE BEFORE the six-year illness that led up to this day when I faced death had been filled with fighting the evils of the prince of this world. I had not heeded the words of my husband, my family, or my friends warning me that I was working too hard and not taking care of myself. I was driven by a yearning to make up for the sins in my life by doing good. There was little time for God, let alone myself or those I loved. The light had gone from my life, replaced by all the sordidness of man's inhumanity to man.

The biggest portion of that time, I had no real relationship with the Lord. And even during the times that I thought I had a relationship with Him, I was mistaken. What I thought that I was, who I thought I was, was nothing, not even remotely as real as the close identity in the Lord that I have today.

Although my life, from the beginning, had been filled with dark periods of circumstances I could not explain, I was ignorant of the devastating presence of the enemy. In my ignorance, I attributed the trials and tragedies of my tumultuous life to either bad luck or, my favorite personnel excuse, coincidence. I was raised as a Lutheran from the moment I was sprinkled as an infant with the ceremonial drops of baptismal water. Somewhere along the way, I began to wander away from religion—for that is what I knew God to be, just "religion"—leading up to the day in my thirties when I completely turned my back on God.

Although my weekly pilgrimages to church and my Monday through Friday Lutheran school education gave me a firm foundation in Biblical words, they failed to penetrate my mind and soul with a meaningful relationship with all that God is. I was blind to the fact that it is either God or Satan that I allowed to control every second of my existence. I was blind to the fact that I had the power to resist or surrender to the prince of the earth at any time. I was well schooled in religion, but I had no earthly—or heavenly— idea that the Holy Spirit was a real entity just a breath of life away, both a powerful weapon against Satan's assaults and a healing comfort ever ready to soothe and comfort my pain. Until recently, I believed that my life had been controlled by some enigmatic force which I had to survive and endure the best way that I could.

Oh yes, I knew to pray to God. I knew to pray to the God of religion. I would reach out to him in anguish at times, reciting the memorized prayers I had been taught, but never once did I actually seek Him. I did not know of this seeking God thing. I saw him as hovering above the clouds somewhere, "out there," watching me down below as I bounced from one relationship to another, one tragedy to another. Not once did I see Him as living inside me, standing beside me. Oh, what a difference it would have made! I had no idea that the Holy Spirit could give me the power to fight against Satan.

To this day I remember an incident when I could not have been more than five or six, an incident which I believe instilled in me the desire to prove myself to be worthy, a drive to succeed.

My paternal grandfather's family was a proud lot. The Americanized version of their name is listed on the rolls at Ellis Island. Back then they wouldn't allow punctuation and pronunciation marks to be included when they entered your name upon the registration sheets; the typewriters were not equipped with them. Your name instantly became something totally different from what it had been; ours went from Müntzer pronounced Mintzer, to Muntzer. The reigning matriarch of the family, my great-grandmother Ottie, had been born in Germany and moved to Indiana when she married my great-grandfather.

I clearly remember this particular day. I was patiently waiting, sitting in the anteroom of the cavernous five-story brick family home, my skinny legs crossed daintily at the ankles, my long braids dangling on my slight shoulders. No smile graced my tiny face, for a smile would have revealed my cavity-filled teeth, the result of thin enamel and being put to bed with a bottle as a baby which often held either orange juice or Coca-

Cola. I never smiled in pictures. In fact, I rarely smiled at all through my childhood.

As the heavy doors of the room slid open and disappeared into the oak-paneled walls, I bravely stepped into the enormous living room which had been turned into my great-grandmother's sick room. There she lay in all her regal splendor. A beige steel hospital bed had been purchased at great expense and served as her throne. Her thin white hair was braided and placed in an oval atop her head like a crown. Her rounded shoulders were draped with a delicately crocheted beige shawl. You could tell that at one time she had been a formidable woman by the way she held her chin high. Her prominent aristocratic nose still assumed an uppity position. Her eyes were tiny slits set in her plump face. Her pencil-thin, clenched lips bore no semblance of a smile.

My knees were knocking as I turned and curtseyed as I had been instructed to do. Her majesty surveyed me up and down, never smiling. With an even loftier upturned nose, she pronounced, "She'll do."

Everyone in the room smiled, causing me to relax my clenched mouth. Oh no, she saw them! I quickly slammed tight my lips, hoping I had not exposed my ugly, cavity-ridden teeth. Then she smiled, or at least it seemed she smiled, making one more pronouncement: "Yes, she'll do—but fix her teeth!"

Years after that day, when I was in my thirties, I remembered my grandmother saying, "You were lucky. Her highness held the belief that all female children should be drowned in gunny sacks like unwanted kittens."

My paternal grandmother's people were also of strong German stock, people of the land, mostly farmers. Ma was an exception. She was trained as a practical nurse and was able to use her skills also taking care of various members of our family throughout her life. She lived two weeks' shy of her ninety-sixth birthday. I spent many hours sitting at Ma's knee, listening to her multitude of rich and colorful tales of our various aunts, uncles, cousins, and the lot.

Ma especially loved to recount stories of her sisters who lived "up in the country," "the country" being the small farming community of Warrenton, Indiana. They all lived in a red-brick farmhouse surrounded by lush cornfields with a huge red barn, a slaughterhouse, and a chicken yard. This picturesque setting was the backdrop for the story which inspired the title of this book.

My oldest daughter attended the same small church-school which my father, my brothers and sister and I, and all of my cousins had attended. Public school buses didn't transport "church school" children, so parents did. It had become routine for me to complete my transportation duties and then drop by Ma's house two or three times a week to check on her and just spend some time with her.

On this particular day, we ate a good ole' country breakfast of fresh side (thick country bacon), eggs, and crisp, lard-fried potatoes, followed by a steaming hot cup of coffee. Then, as usual, we carried a final cup of brew into the living room. Ma backed up to her state-of-the-art electronic recliner (we affectionately named this her "butt-jacking chair"), carefully leaned back against a crocheted cushion, and got seated. (Years of hard work as a practical nurse had taken its toll on her body.)

As she sat rubbing both of her aching knees in smooth circular motions, gazing out her picture window, I had a question for her.

"Ma, what do you mean when you say that you are 'killin' snakes'?" I had heard her too many times to count utter those words and had begun reciting this mantra myself.  Today I wanted to know what those words meant.

She smiled, her eyes twinkling and her knee-rubbing growing more intense.  She let out one of her deep sighs, leaned back, and began to tell me what at the time seemed like an amusing and quaint family tale.

Little did I know that this story would have a profound effect on my life and give meaning to the tribulations which would soon begin to envelop me.

As she set the scene for this particular story, she directed my thoughts back to the family farm. Her description carried me to the kitchen of the farmhouse and me lighting down at the large rectangular dining table that had been the setting for the delicious down-home meals our family had enjoyed for generations.

Ma began to tell me of how, in the old days, the women of the family participated in all aspects of farm life. I had only seen my great-aunts care for the chickens and carry out "women's work." My great-great-aunts did it all. As Ma remembered it, one of those great-great-aunts often took to the fields to carry out her assigned task of plowing in preparation for planting. She could be seen out the small window that looked out over the side yard past the driveway and on into one of the cornfields, which continued on to the pond where generations of cousins would fish, swim, frog-gig, and ice-skate as children. As she spun her tale, I could distinctly see this strong, tall woman clothed in a long, unpretentious dress. probably made from flour sacks, the kind with rosettes printed on it. I imagined this woman's long apron blowing in the wind as she toiled in the field. Ma related to me how she could be seen out that window determinedly marching along behind the plow horse, guiding the wood and metal plow.

As she made sure that the rows were even and straight, she appeared from a distance, at random intervals, to be grasping a whip in one hand and holding the reins with the other. This happened time and time again. It was confusing to the family members because she did not carry a whip into the field nor did the horse appear to be slowing his pace before the onslaught of whipping. Confusing—unless you knew what was actually occurring. What appeared to be an unwarranted whipping of an undeserving animal was, in reality, snake-killing.

As she was trekking through the fields, churning up the soil beneath her blade, occasionally she would unearth a snake. Now, this could have been a harmless garden snake or a northern copperhead, Indiana's most common poisonous snake. Many species inhabited the terrain. No matter the variety, she would simply bend over, grab the snake by the tail, and with a flick of her wrist, pop it in mid-air, breaking its spine. No muss, no fuss, just another pest taken care of. Never missing a beat, she continued with the plowing as if she were swatting a fly. She exhibited no fear, no female shrieks of horror. She simply had to take care of business and carry on with the task at hand. She never let a mere snake keep her from the work before her.

Anyone who witnessed this scenario for the first time would invariably ask, "What is she doing out there?" The answer was, "*Ach du Lieber* [Oh my God]! She's just killin' snakes again." Thus, the birth of the phrase which would be handed down through generations of the women in my family.

Whenever one of our women would be working hard, going at it, whether it be cleaning house, reprimanding children, or, in my case, fighting politics to give birth to a women's shelter, if asked what we are doing, our answer was usually, "Just killin' snakes."

I left Ma's house that day filled with a sense of pride about how strong and determined the women in our family were and also with a feeling of connection, a belonging to something important. A sense of identity.

I also remember reading another story once about plowing, the one about the farmer who, in his early years of instruction in plowing, was advised to set his eye on something a little farther away at the end of the furrow. As he was guiding his horse-drawn blade, he fixed his gaze not on a tree but upon a cow. That cow became his focus. He moved along, not paying attention to anything other than that cow. When he turned at the end of the row, he saw that his row had veered off to the side. He squinted at the object of his concentration and found that he had not noticed that the cow had been slowly moving. What he had focused on to keep him in line, could not be counted on. His furrow had become crooked.

Much like that farmer, I took my eye off of all I had been taught to be true. I looked away from God for only a moment, a moment which would forever alter the course of my life.

When we do not set our focus on God, the only One who will never change or move from us, we lose our direction. Our crooked path leads us into destruction. When we take our focus off of God, we will encounter snakes. If we focus on the snake, we will never accomplish what God has ordained for us to do.

If Satan's ploys take our focus off of Jesus and His will for us, we risk being bitten. In a dry and desolate time in my life, I took my focus off of God and directed my attention to the world. And just like in Acts 28, when Paul reached into the woodpile and the poisonous snake latched onto his hand, I reached out my hand and allowed Satan to pierce my life and inject his poison.

His power of selection and seduction is precise and powerful. His sole purpose is to steal, kill, and destroy every living creature on earth. He seeks and then zeros in on his victims with laser-like accuracy. When he detects a weakness, he uses it as a point of entry where he employs all of his resources—his knowledge of who we have been and knowledge of how God is using us at the moment. He uses all of this to develop just the right strategic weapon to kill and destroy our purpose in God's Kingdom.

But he is not invincible; he has a natural enemy, a foe, someone he fears. Even a snake has an archenemy, a predator—the mongoose. The mongoose is not afraid of the snake because he knows that the way he was created with a thick, furry coat and lightning-quick speed allows him to be virtually untouchable by the snake. The same mechanism which allows a snake to detect its nemesis the mongoose has been incorporated into the mongoose and allows it to have a keen sense of awareness of the presence of a snake.

God has equipped each believer with the capacity to detect and sense the evil workings of Satan. For most, it will lie dormant for a lifetime. Our warning device is called "discernment." In order to activate and use this ability properly, we must first be filled with the power of the Holy Spirit.

I was ignorant of this capability. I only knew the Holy Spirit as the third person of the Trinity. My early religious education provided a yearly Happy-Birthday-Holy-Spirit kind of relationship each time the observance of Pentecost rolled around. After that, he was put back in a box, along with the paper flame headbands worn that day in Sunday school. I believed that the promptings I felt or heard in my mind were woman's intuition or just an overactive conscience.

Without a relationship or understanding of this powerful presence of God, I felt like a pinball inside a machine full of flippers, bumpers, and holes. For the six years of illness leading up to my encounter with God in the recovery room, my life was lived in a constant state of Tilt, with soul-deafening background noise of a scoreboard tallying Satan's attacks upon me.

Now here, in a coma in the hospital, God was commissioning me to join Him in "cleaning up this earth." Although the years before my illness had been filled with battling the worst of Satan's workings, I had been doing that in my own strength. Now there began in me a new sense of purpose. God had given me a glimpse of this new direction for my life in the visions during the coma. The direction my life had taken prior to this point in time, this fight for my life had taken me down quite a different path.

# CHAPTER 3

## THE CHARMING SERPENT

Psalm 58:3–5 NIV

> Even from birth the wicked go astray; from the womb they are wayward, spreading lies. Their venom is like the venom of a snake, like that of a cobra that has stopped its ears, that will not heed the tune of the charmer, however skillful the enchanter may be.

**SATAN'S POWER TO CHARM** us into believing his lies was the first weapon he used against Eve in the garden. Just as with all of us, Satan began chasing me early on in my life.

Actual snake charmers use a flutelike instrument called a pungi. Contrary to popular belief, it is not the music that hypnotizes a snake but the swaying movement of the flute. In our lives, it is **Satan who tries to hypnotize us into dancing to his tune.** He can speak disguised as the most seductive, welcoming voice we have unfortunately ever heard.  His voice may come from within a person who at first seems the answer to all of our insecurities and hopes for the future.  He is cunning.  But just as the snake charmers were often called to rid a home of the venomous creature, we Christians possess the ability to call on the Holy Spirit to rid our lives of the pestilent Satan.  We can call on the Holy Spirit to put an end to our torment.  If we truly believe, He will answer our call.

For the majority of my life, I had no idea who the Holy Spirit is or of his power to protect me from the evil that lay hidden before me.  I had no idea that He could or would actually speak to me.  My education in religion was traditional and conservative.  Ma had made it a point to profess her association with her particular religion and, when describing an acquaintance, would sometimes say that they were a nice person and then whisper "…but they were Catholic," or "…Baptist," or whatever.

When Scripture warns young men and women not to become unequally yoked to a non-believer, the lines established are very easy to discern.  It's simple. If the person is not a Christian, do not date that person, and do not marry that person. However, I was totally unprepared to be watchful for a person who purported to be a Christian but wasn't. I listened to Satan's voice through a man-child as he enticed me to join him in a lifestyle I had once abhorred.

My education about sexual matters was rudimentary at best.  This subject was never discussed with me by any grown-up.  I discovered what it meant to "have sex" rather abruptly one fall morning in homeroom my freshman year in high school. My desk-mate assumed the honor of explaining to me in great detail exactly how "it" was carried out. My response, uttered in an almost convulsive groan, was, "No way, never, I'll never do that!"

One morning, also during my freshman year in high school, my homeroom teacher was sharing his thoughts on dating. He stated that we might be surprised as to whom we eventually would choose to marry. He mused that it might just be the person furthest from our thoughts at this time in our lives. As I began to go over the many prospective suitors available at my school, my thoughts settled on one boy in particular. He was a well-known drinker, a football player, a member of the school choir, and of somewhat questionable moral background. He went to church; he was raised Baptist. His father had worked with my father at one of the steel plants in our hometown. There were rumors of all sorts of escapades. I remember thinking of him—he would be my never-in-a-million-years-would-I-marry person.

It would be only four years later, while we both attended the same university, that this same boy entered my life when he was chosen to be my partner in a scholarship vocal group. We were attracted to one another. The little girl from a small church-school was totally enamored that someone who had been one of the popular kids in high school was now interested in her. He was clever, Robert Redford good-looking, and smooth. As they say, he could have sold ice cubes to Eskimos, a real silver-tongued devil. Somehow I forgot that he was my, oh-no-not-in-a-million-years person. I had no idea at the time that not only would he be my musical partner in college but that he would soon become my first husband.

This boy was a member of a fraternity, and that life centered on drinking, partying, and, of course, sex. I had managed to hold at bay the latter of these vices until midway through my freshmen year of college when I accepted his proposal of marriage. Once the ring was on my finger, I convinced myself that it was now permissible to sleep with him. After all, this was the seventies. I had the right to "share the love." The world told me so (Satan's favorite voice, the world). I was oblivious to the ramifications of my choice. Casting aside all that I had been programmed to believe, I assumed that the green light had flashed, granting me permission to give myself to my fiancé. I ignored and buried down deep inside me the caution light which God had placed in my conscience.

The guilt I felt over this transgression drove me to marry a man I did not love and sometimes hated. I had to marry him to be a good little girl. I believed God couldn't forgive me unless I did something to receive His forgiveness. I heard Satan's voice as it spoke to me, convicting me of what I had done wrong. I did not listen to or seek God's voice, His Grace. I never knew that I could so easily accept His unconditional forgiveness.

I began what for me became a way of life, thinking that I had to do something drastic to prove my repentance. I had to prove that I was a good girl, worthy. I did not know that just as Satan speaks his lies to us, God speaks His truth, that He speaks to us in various ways, His voice bringing messages of healing, hope, and also warnings of imminent danger.

God spoke words of warning to me through the flames of a candle on my wedding day, just as I was joining my life to another in deceit. As the wedding march began, I looked down at my off-white gown; I had chosen ivory instead of pure white because in my heart I felt unworthy to wear pure white. I was not pure.

When I had begun looking for the perfect dress for the occasion, I had recalled a Pennsylvania Dutch joke that Ma, my grandmother, had told me. The story goes that this unmarried lady was planning her funeral. When the undertaker asked her what garment she would like to be buried in, she asked, "So what are they wearing these days?" to which he explained that for a woman who had never been married or "anything," he had a lovely white shroud and that for a woman who had been married there was a beautiful purple one. After great thought, she replied, "Just give me a white one with a few splotches of purple!" At the time she told me that story, I thought that it was funny. When I was faced with the truth of my status as no longer a virgin, the laughter ceased; what remained was only guilt and shame.

As I stood at the ornate, gilded altar of the church where I had been baptized and then confirmed, resplendent in my pristine ivory gown, clutching the wedding taper which my mother had lit at the beginning of the ceremony, God spoke to me through the flame. My heart was full of shame and resentment for the man I had just promised to love, honor, and obey. His drinking had already caused misery in my life. The reconstructed automobile he was driving was a result of a head-on with a telephone- pole drunk-driving episode. I resented this boy who had, in a drunken outburst, almost succeeded in causing our wedding reception to be canceled at the local union hall just days before the ceremony. My thoughts raced to the week ahead and my plans to obtain an annulment of this marriage.

As I reached to my right to light the unity candle, I heard my brother, one of five groomsmen, let out an audible gasp. From the corner of my eye, I could barely see his body move as he lunged towards me. The sound of his gasp and his frantic movement startled me into the realization that I was about to set my wedding veil on fire. The flames left a faint black blemish on the candlelight netting, a prophetic etching of what would just a few years later, become an actual event.

The wedding veil was intended to represent the purity of the bride. I was not pure. I had relinquished that title two years before. Another definition of a veil is, a thing that conceals, disguises, or obscures something. I was concealing the truth to a church full of family and friends. The disguise I wore could not hide the truth from God. The hate in my heart, the lie I had just uttered there at the altar, was not concealed from God by a white dress or veil. The veiled truth was that I had lied.

I should have listened to God's warning to me. I should have had the courage to stop the lie right there at the altar of God's church. But I was weak. I interpreted with my human reasoning that I had to go through with this atrocity. Had I known then that this was but a glimpse of a time when fire would play a major role in my life and marriage and that God was warning me in a not-so-subtle fashion to walk away from this life not blessed by him—oh had I listened? If only I had possessed the courage. If only I had listened to His voice through the warning flame. Instead I let the serpent's hiss continue whispering to me that I must keep up this charade.

Possibly had I looked deep into the light of the unity candle, I might have seen the figure of a serpent dancing in the flames. If I had listened above the sounds of my gasping brother, might I have heard the hiss of Satan the snake?

# CHAPTER 4

## THE FIERY SERPENT

THIS PORTION OF MY LIFE felt to me like a punishment, the punishment I deserved for my lie at the altar. Numbers 21:6, NIV, says: "And the Lord sent fiery serpents among the people, and they bit the people; and much of the people of Israel died." God sent the fiery serpents as a punishment to the children of Israel because they had been ungrateful for God's grace and favor. I had done something much worse than being ungrateful to God: I had knowingly lied to God in a pledge, at His altar.

Satan is mentioned fifty-nine times in the Bible by any number of names other than Satan or serpent. One of the names might include "leviathan." Leviathan has many different interpretations in Scripture, but Job 41:18-21, NIV, says: "Its snorting throws out flashes of light; its eyes are like the rays of dawn. Flames stream from its mouth; sparks of fire shoot out. Smoke pours from its nostrils as from a boiling pot over burning reeds. Its breath sets coals ablaze, and flames dart from its mouth."

This is the fiery leviathan I was about to face.

Ten days after graduation from college, when we had been married for a year (a marriage I had not had annulled, of course), I discovered that I was pregnant. My husband had not planned on having a baby so soon. That did not fit into his plan for the future. He had banked on the idea that I would obtain a teaching job when I graduated to supplement what he made as a clothing-store manager. He wanted to start making the "big bucks" as quickly as possible. We were hard pressed for money to pay for an unexpected pregnancy, so he devised a plan to obtain some big money quickly.

Sometime during my senior year of college, midway through our first year of marriage, we had purchased a small cabin cruiser; an old German make called a Luger Cruiser. It needed a lot of repairs, which we completed together. However, our friends had larger, more expensive boats, so, in my husband's view, our tiny boat didn't measure up. My husband liked money, and he liked to appear that he had more than he actually did. Appearances were very important to him.

The boat had become a source of frustration for him. The transom of the tiny vessel was never adequate to support the heavy load of the outboard motor. The transom had weakened with age and was in danger of separating itself from the rest of the boat. It had become even more unstable during a boating misadventure when the propeller of the motor hit a submerged log, a frequent hazard on the treacherous

Ohio River. We had filed an insurance claim and with the reimbursement procured the necessary repairs. I believe that this was the inception of his arson idea—insurance.

How ironic that in the not so distant future he would secure a position with an insurance company. How appropriate that this boat, which did not possess a firm foundation and was incapable of providing the necessary support for moving forward, would mirror the fact that our marriage was not founded on solid ground and would be incapable of surviving the treacherous rivers of our lives.

It was July 1974, a year into our marriage. My husband informed me that it was going to happen on this particular evening. He had told our friends and some of our family what he planned to do. God spoke to me all that day warning me of what was to come. I did not know that it was God speaking.

Early that morning, I had read a newspaper article describing a newly discovered treatment for burn victims. A young man had been terribly burned by a jet-fuel explosion. His severe burns were healed with a combination of soaking in highly concentrated chlorine water followed by what was termed "debriding." The man in the article had experienced a miraculous scar-reduced recovery due to the fact that the debriding removed the damaged top layers of skin and allowed the burns to heal from the bottom up.

A warning voice inside my head said, "Stop him."

My maternal grandmother, who was with me as I read the story, began to recount her tale of how she had used what in her day was called "chlorazine water" while treating the almost fatal burns of my uncle, her son.

Again I heard a voice: "Stop him". I felt powerless to stop him.

That evening, around 10:30, he left our living room with the parting statement, "I'm going to do it."

I begged and pleaded with him, "Please don't. Please don't. Something bad is going to happen."

He cursed me and slammed the front door.

I sat motionless on the sofa, staring into space and engulfed in eerie silence. It seemed like hours until he once again entered the living room.

"I need you to help me," he barked in an almost guttural noise. He wanted me to go down into the belly of the boat and hold open a valve.

I was terrified. Every instinct I had said to run. But I was frozen. I pleaded again with him to stop. He cursed me even louder and again disappeared out the door.

The silence seemed to last forever. The stillness of time, which I now know is when God is speaking to me, was deafening. Then everything became light. I could see the orange-red glow of the flames as they danced into view through the kitchen window. The silence was pierced by repetitive explosions—and then the screams. They seemed to be coming from somewhere not real, horrifying, deep inside screams; wounded animal sounds.

I leapt up from my state of suspended animation and burst through the front door (the heat emanating from the kitchen warned me that going through the back door was impossible). From this point on everything seemed to be happening in slow motion. I remember a random thought that it was like the scenes in the *Six-Million-Dollar Man*. But this was really happening. It had really happened. What God had warned me about on our wedding day and what He had given me a glimpse of just that very day was happening.

The image of what I saw will never leave my memory. At first, it appeared as though a portion of the boat had broken away and was hurtling through the air. But it was not a piece of the boat—it was my husband running towards me entirely engulfed in flames. Directly behind him, I could see the inferno which was once our tiny boat. As he ran, the flames danced against the still, black night.

He dropped to the asphalt driveway and began to roll in agony. The only thing I could remember was the mantra I, and all pre-911 emergency-call children had been taught--dial O for the operator and tell her the emergency. Now I myself seemed to be operating in slow motion. I felt as if I were floating up the front porch steps and in one uninterrupted motion went from the door to standing in front of the avocado green kitchen wall phone, placing my index finger in the 0 and running it around the dial.

The operator's monotone voice said, "Operator. May I help you?" It was returned by my out- of-context calm reply, "We've had a fire and an explosion," and followed with our address.

Her now irritated tone resonated with, "I'm sorry. I cannot take that information. You'll have to dial [blah blah blah]."

"Here listen," I said, and held the phone so she could hear the screams from outside. The next sound I heard was sirens piercing the night. I could see the intermittent red glow of flashing lights through the screened front door.

I ran out the door and onto the tiny concrete front stoop. The horror of what lay before me finally sank in. I watched as rescue workers hovered like so many bees over what looked like a huge white shaking cocoon. A neighbor two doors down from our house was a volunteer firefighter. Upon hearing the explosion and the screams of anguish, he had instinctively wet down a bed sheet and rushed to the scene, immediately encasing my husband's body with the cloth, extinguishing the flames and ultimately saving his life.

My trembling legs finally gave way. I tumbled down the steps into a mass of convulsing agony. I was shaking so severely that my neighbor had to cover my body with hers to calm my spasms. One crimson rescue vehicle after another converged on the scene. Huge hoses began showering both our house and our neighbor's. I would not discover until days later that both houses suffered scarring from the flames

When the emergency workers assessed the injuries to my husband, they discovered that his left arm had suffered a compound fracture, the protruding bones a result of impact with our neighbor's fence when he was blown from the craft. I thought it rather odd that when the ambulance arrived, I was placed in the back of it and my husband's swaddled body was seated in the front seat between the two attendants. I later learned that they had realized that they had to keep him alert to prevent him from slipping into a coma. They had mere minutes to transport him to the hospital before renal failure would set in. I was put in the ambulance too because they were afraid that I was losing my baby. I was only three months into the pregnancy, a critical time for such a trauma. It would not be revealed until my daughter was almost two years old exactly how traumatic this event had been.

    A Medivac helicopter had been summoned and was on standby to rush him to the burn unit of Barnes Hospital in St. Louis, but his doctors didn't think he would survive the trip. He had suffered first, second, and third-degree burns over eighty percent of his body. His eyes had been saved by his reflex to protect his face from the blast by covering them with his right forearm. He had inhaled some of the flames, but luckily the direct contact with the flames had stopped just short of reaching his throat and lungs. At the time of the explosion, he had been wearing only jean cutoffs and tennis shoes. Those were the only areas of his body not touched by the flames. He was lucky to be alive.

    The hatred which had begun at the scene of the fire welled up inside me with a feeling so intense that it frightened me. The snake Satan, the fiery serpent, had found the crack he needed to enter into my life on a level I had never imagined. Hate breeds hate. It will eat away at your soul until you are but a shadow of who you once were.

I was given some sort of medication in the emergency room and then wheeled by my mother-in-law into the room where they were treating my husband. We were given instructions to say our goodbyes to him. He was not expected to survive the impending surgery. He looked like a giant burnt marshmallow.

I hated that object lying on the table. It didn't look human. I saw the results of greed and selfishness displayed before me in a form which had no resemblance to a human being. The X-ray technician summoned to attend to him had been a classmate of ours in high school. She later told me that she worked on him for quite a number of minutes before she had recognized him. Not until she looked at his name on the chart did she realize that this mound of charred flesh was indeed the person she knew to be my husband.

For the first time in my life, I defiantly turned to God in heaven and uttered these words, "Why, God?" Not "Why, God, did this happen to him?" but "Why, God, is he still alive when they are telling me I might lose my baby? Why is he still alive when he did this abominable thing?"

At the time I never gave a thought to our wedding day. I was not the person that I am today. I had not the slightest inkling that the flames of the unity candle scorching the delicate netting of my wedding veil, the wedding veil which was supposed to represent purity, was the Holy Spirit speaking words of warning to me. I now know that it was the Holy Spirit screaming to me there in God's house, "Don't do this thing." I stood there in front of God and three hundred witnesses and lied. I had promised a vow I never intended to keep. I had pledged to love, honor, and obey a man I despised. There are consequences of such a lie, consequences which would follow me for many years to come.

The ensuing weeks were filled with regular visits to stand by his bedside in the intensive-care unit. Because he was such a heavy drinker, the doctors requested that I bring to the hospital a cooler containing beer. They cautioned that his body could not endure the withdrawal from alcohol while it was battling all of the various traumas it had received. This Baptist hospital requested that I bring a cooler of beer into its intensive-care unit.

When he was released from intensive care into a regular private room, he was extremely agitated. He would only become calm if I stayed in the room with him, so his hospital room became my room, day and night, for over a month. The tiny cot they placed beside his bed where I slept felt as if it was a coffin and I was trapped inside unable to breathe, a coffin I had to share with a man I detested but had to care for in sickness and in health. I had promised.

Mechanical deodorizing machines had to be placed throughout that floor of the hospital because the stench was so horrific. You could smell it even two floors below, the smell of burnt flesh.

This was my life for two months. Be the dutiful wife and hold in the anger. Hold in the hatred. I prayed to God to protect my baby, but I didn't pray to God to heal my husband.

He survived, but the weeks following the explosion were filled with weekly trips to therapy where he was soaked in whirlpool baths of chlorine water, followed by surgery where his burned flesh was debrided to allow the wounds to heal with minimal scarring, just as I had read in the newspaper on the morning of the fire. The Holy Spirit had warned me. The Holy Spirit through me had warned him. I had begged him not to do this thing. He did not listen to my voice or to the words the Holy Spirit had spoken to me. At this time in my life, I was oblivious that the voice I had heard was the Holy Spirit. I called it a premonition. The world calls it that.

I continued to stuff all of these feelings of hatred deep down inside of me. After all, I had to take care of him. I had to bathe him and feed him, tie his shoes, clean up his messes. I had promised for better or worse to God. I had promised. I kept the anger in as I had learned to do as a child. I wanted to scream, "He did this. He did this to himself." I kept the screams inside. I kept inside me the knowledge that he had brought this torment upon himself. I kept it inside me that he had done this to me and possibly injured his unborn child. The snake, the serpent of hatred, began to eat at my soul.

At this point in my life, I knew nothing of the thing called the spirit of leviathan. As I was conducting research for this book, I googled the word leviathan and was taken to the Christian Connection website where I learned that the Leviathan Spirit is found in three books of the Bible, Job, Isaiah and Psalms. I am not delving into naming spirits, but the descriptions of this spirit I found there seemed to fit, particularly the part about pride, worldliness, self-centeredness, and self-exaltation.

I believe that the fiery serpent leviathan, through greed and pride, had pierced my husband's being and those sins were now being used to levy an attack upon him and upon me. I believe that the spirit of hatred, another of the evil one's minions, was taking a foothold in my life and waging war inside my heart. I had never read Isaiah 27: "In that day, the Lord will punish with his sword—his fierce, great and powerful sword—leviathan the gliding serpent, leviathan the coiling serpent; he will slay the monster of the sea." I was yoked to a living breathing leviathan spirit inside of my husband. Leviathan had twisted and turned my husband into a creature of his design, and now the serpent Satan was using his tool of hatred to chip away at my soul.

The creature the rattlesnake is usually predictable. In most cases, it will warn you of its presence before it attacks. The serpent's warning device sends out an unmistakable sound which strikes fear into the hearts of anyone who hears it. The Holy Spirit also sends warnings when the serpent Satan is about to strike. The Holy Spirit tried to warn me that day, but I felt helpless to stop the madness.

Some people believe in omens; I believe that God often sends us signs and warnings to prevent us from making disastrous mistakes. I know that God provided me with the opportunity to remove myself from an unholy union. At the altar, when my wedding veil almost caught fire, I do believe that He was warning me of the gravity of what I was about to do. I could have removed myself from proceeding with a marriage to a man I detested. I could have prevented the situation I now found myself in. Instead, I stood at the altar of God and lied. I had promised to love, honor, and obey a man I did not love. I went ahead with a ceremony of marriage, an institution sanctioned by God, which I knew to be based on a lie. In my distorted view of Christianity, I felt that I had to marry the man I had given my physical body to in order to be a "good Christian girl." I had stood there repeating vows when in my heart I was plotting to pursue an annulment the very next week.

When he was finally able to go home, my days were filled with feeding him, dressing him and changing his bandages; perfect training for the baby on the way.

His physical body would take months to heal but his spiritual being was different following one of his surgeries, he asked to speak to the pastor of our church. I was not present for this discussion but something happened during the pastor's visit, something totally unexpected, that day he asked to join the church.

From that day and for the next few years, he seemed to have changed. I remember one day watching him, under Ma's sink, dressed in a three-piece suit, fixing a busted pipe. He was caring and thoughtful. His usual demeanor of arrogant confidence had also softened. I wondered if his close brush with death was responsible. He attended Lamaze child-birth classes with me. On one such occasion we entered the hospital through the emergency room, me pregnant and him all bandaged up using a cane to walk. We were immediately meet by a nurse with a wheelchair. I thought that she had assumed that I was in labor but she had taken one look at him and thought that he had come for treatment.

My beautiful baby girl was born that January. God is good. The first time I held her was the first time I knew what real love is. In an instant my life made sense. Life was good.

When she was a year and one month old, I found out I was pregnant with my second child. Three months into the pregnancy, I went into labor, but, thank the Lord, the doctors were able to stop the contractions with intravenous alcohol. The doctors and I fought to keep her alive through monthly episodes of early labor, each time requiring the IV's of alcohol, a common practice in the seventies prior to the discovery of fetal alcohol syndrome.

My second beautiful daughter was delivered prematurely at eight months, a healthy six pounds. Now I had two gifts from God to love. God is good.

When it was time to take her to the pediatrician for her six weeks' check-up, my new baby girl thankfully checked out just fine, but I asked the doctor to take a look at my oldest daughter, explaining something odd I had observed in her physical development: I had noticed that when she would move her left hand, her right hand would move also. She never reached for anything with her right hand, and she seemed to fall a lot more than other children her age. She was 22 months old.

He manipulated her right hand and foot for a moment and asked if he could be excused to take her for further examination. It seemed like forever. As I sat there clutching my tiny new infant, my thoughts raced. What was wrong? What was taking so long?

After about one hour, he returned. He said, "Mama, sit down. We need to talk. We seem to have a case of cerebral palsy."

I wanted to scream. Having no concrete knowledge of the condition, I pictured her in a wheelchair, progressively getting worse. He assured me that her condition would always remain as it was at that time. He explained that it was brain damage which resulted in her muscular difficulties.

When I gave the news to my husband that night, he reacted in a rather peculiar manner. He said that we weren't going to tell anyone about her condition, absolutely no one, not even our parents.

We were referred to a neurologist, who confirmed the diagnosis. He said that after he had gone over the records of my pregnancy and her delivery, he felt certain that the injury occurred when I fell down the front steps the night of the fire.

I vaguely remembered the words of a Bible verse I had once been required to memorize in Lutheran school, something about the result of the sins of the father being visited to the next generations.

# CHAPTER 5

## THE FLEEING SERPENT

Job 26:13 NIV

By His breath the heavens became fair; His hand has pierced the fleeing serpent.

LIFE BEGAN TO TAKE ON a rather predictable routine after my daughter's premature birth, even with her constant trips in and out of the hospital with asthma attacks. My father-in-law suffered several heart attacks, and we seemed to live in waiting rooms of hospitals. My husband had given up selling insurance and had been running an independent oil company which was owned by one of his former clients.  His worldly craving for more and more money and status had increased to extreme levels. It seemed as though nothing or anyone was more important than money. Of course, this meant that we needed a bigger and better house. We hadn't sold the one we lived in yet, but that didn't seem to matter, we purchased a new one anyway.

We had also joined the local country club some years earlier, initially so that our oldest daughter could utilize the swimming pool, which the doctor had recommended as the perfect therapy for her physical condition. "The club" was directly across the street from our home, and it was significantly cheaper to join it than to build a pool of our own. The position in the community that this afforded us merely fed leviathan's need for self-importance.

I enjoyed taking the girls for a swim and visiting with the "regular" mothers who also used the pool as a great means of exercise for their children. Both girls became members of the swim team. We couldn't afford the expensive treats for our children sold at the snack bar, so we would sneak in fruit drinks and goodies. We were definitely not members of the country-club set.

For a time after the fire and his recovery, my husband had sought a closer relationship with God, or so I had hoped. He had asked to speak with our pastor and had begun taking a greater interest in church. But the status of belonging to a country club was like a drug to him. He began to revel in the class distinction that mixing with the well-to-do provided. We were not wealthy by any means, but he pretended to all that we were.

I remember a particular shopping trip with my girls. We had fun trying on fancy dresses which we couldn't afford. We would play dress-up that way. After one such excursion, my oldest mentioned to her daddy that mommy had tried on the prettiest dress. He growled, "What did it look like? How much did it cost?" I said that it was nice but way out of our price range. He arrogantly responded that maybe I should buy the dress; after all, I needed to look the part of an oilman's wife. That was how he saw the world. The girls and I were there to make him look good.

In the New American Standard Bible, Job says this about leviathan: "His strong scales are his pride, shut up as with a tight seal."

Solomon has been paraphrased as saying, "Pride goeth before a fall." The time of our fall was soon upon us.

The house across from the country club was soon replaced with a much larger, newer version. Again we moved into a new house before selling the old one. I worked feverishly redecorating the five-thousand-square-foot custom-built home we had purchased. I had painted, wallpapered, dyed carpets and made curtains for the entire house. It was beautiful. The girls had a playroom on the lower level that was twenty feet by twenty feet. Their bedroom's looked like they jumped from the pages of Better Homes and Gardens magazine. The girls had a fairytale existence. I began to immerse myself in carpools, Brownie troop meetings, sewing, and baking, anything that would divert my attention from the reality of my existence. My faith consisted of going to church on Sunday. My Bible lay unopened somewhere in a random drawer. Our oldest was enjoying Lutheran school while the youngest attended a Methodist pre-school. It looked like we were Christians, but our relationship with God was purely social.

It was one week before Mother's Day almost eleven years into our marriage. My husband had gone to

Houston, Texas, for the Offshore Oil Show. He was staying with his company's owner in his million-dollar home on the Street of Dreams. I remember I had baked brownies for him to enjoy on the long drive from Indiana. When he returned early on a Saturday morning, he wouldn't look me in the eye. He didn't even acknowledge the "Welcome home, Daddy" sign the girls had made for him. Instead, he immediately went downstairs to his office. Later that day I remarked to my father that something was strange but I wasn't sure what. My husband stayed drunk for most of the next twenty-four hours.

Sunday was Mother's Day. Of course, we had to have brunch at the club. My father and step-mother joined us to celebrate the day. My husband was drinking even more than usual. At one point he turned to my father and, gesturing towards the girls and me, asked him what he would do if tomorrow he had to take care of all three of these girls. Of course, Dad thought he was joking and said that he didn't know, he would probably run for the hills. Later I would find out that he had told several men at the club just what he was planning to do. It was he, not my father, who was planning to run for the hills.

Early Monday morning, after I had put the girls into their respective carpools, I returned to my bedroom. My husband was throwing his clothes into a suitcase. He shouted at me that I could have the houses, the cars, and the kids. He said, "I'm outta here!"

The same feeling of a slow-motion dream like the one I had experienced the night of the fire began to overtake me. I had no idea where he was going or exactly what had just happened, but I will never forget the overwhelming sense of freedom I felt as I heard the door slam as he left. The words "free at last, free at last," began to repeat over and over in my mind.

I had never read the scripture in Job 26:13, or if I had, I had not paid attention. I know that the original word used in Hebrew for the word "serpent" can be interpreted several ways. The interpretation which has resonated with me as I look back on this time is the one referring to Satan, the great dragon, the serpent. I remember this great sense of freedom that a heavy presence had left my home. I have since learned of the power of evil spirits and how they can inhabit a home. That day I know that the evil inside of my husband did flee. The piercing of that spirit was up to God. I was free.

Sitting for a bit, dazed and alone in the massive empty house, I telephoned my father. After listening to my story of the last two hours, he proposed that maybe my husband was just having a drunken fit. I knew it was more serious. Being my father, he advised me to call my bank to get a handle on what my financial situation was. I called the bank and discovered that my husband had emptied all of our accounts, even the investment account. Alarmed, I raced to his office downstairs, where I found the checkbook and a stack of bills. Among the piles of paper, I found shut-off notices for our gas and electric services. There were mounds of past-due bills. We were penniless, and it seemed we owed money to everyone.

My father and step-mother immediately came over. He totaled up the utility bills and said that he would take care of them. He advised me to immediately seek the counsel of an attorney. He was right: I needed help.

This was the Monday before my thirty-second birthday. The following week was filled with lawyer appointments and calls to and from creditors. He hadn't been paying the bills for quite some time. His house of cards was tumbling down around us. I was advised by the lawyer to find out where he had gone. I had no idea.

One morning that same week, the owner of the oil company came to retrieve some of his equipment from my husband's field truck. He seemed very angry. He informed me that my husband had been drunk that last week in the field and had made a bad call as to how to treat one of his wells. His decision had completely ruined the well, one which had been producing oil for twenty years. He was angry.

The man asked me if I knew where my husband had gone. When I replied no, he began to recount a story of what he had observed the week of the oil show in Houston. He said that while they were visiting a hospitality suite hosted by a man and his daughter, owners of one of the multi-million dollar companies that produced offshore equipment, the conversation had drifted to something along the lines of that if someone were to go after the goose that laid the golden egg, someone just might go after the daughter of the owner of that multimillion-dollar company. She was forty, divorced, with no children, and a millionaire in her own right.

Upon hearing this fortune-hunting scenario, my husband took off his wedding ring, put it in his pocket, and made a beeline for the woman. According to the story, my husband had created a web of lies which he began to spin to the woman, lies about how his wife and son had been killed in an automobile accident and that he was a widower. She bought this line of seduction and followed him into an adulterous rendezvous. The rest of the details were sketchy, but the man went on to say that my husband had later confessed to her and her parents that he had lied about being a widower but that their daughter was so beautiful, he just couldn't resist her. Her mother had said, "Well, at least he's honest!"

The man then chuckled that it was an accepted practice among oil men to have an affair or a girlfriend, but it was not all right to abandon your wife and kids; that just wasn't right.

I was in shock. I lived on valium and Double Colas (the local beverage favorite) for the next few days. I didn't turn to God for help or comfort. I felt that God had abandoned me. I had tried to live by God's rules. I had tried to make things right. I felt that I had paid my penance for my deception by nursing back to health the husband I did not love. Where was God in all this? Must I continue to pay for the lie at the altar?

The next few details are going to sound as though they leaped directly from the pages of a script from Dallas, the popular TV show at the time. The heroine of the melodrama's name was Sue Ellen, and my name was Sue. The villain of the show held the same name as the current villain in my personal soap opera, my husband. The setting for my story, however, was Houston although later I would find that the plot would broaden to a community just outside Dallas. It was all too bizarre, and the saga was about to take on an even greater resemblance to the famous debauchery of the TV show.

According to Amanda Sagan, volunteer educator for Center for Snake Conservation, Snakes are solitary creatures by nature. The only times snakes travel together is either as a mating pair or two or more males searching for a female to mate with. I had the misfortune to be the target of two desperately evil male human serpents with a propensity for mating; the one I was married to and the man who he worked for.

The man who owned the oil company my husband was running and his wife had become like family. We had spent many hours with them in their home and socially. I had heard that the man had a reputation with the ladies, but I had not personally seen that side of him. His wife and I were close. During this time when I was trying to get back on my feet, trying to put together the jigsaw puzzle my life had become, I would occasionally go to various places with the wife. On one such occasion, I was to meet her at her home to go to lunch. My girls were in school, so I was looking forward to the occasion.

I arrived at her house on time, but she had not made it home from another appointment yet. The man welcomed me at the door. I had no qualms about being there with him alone in his home. But, something was not right. You know that feeling you get in the pit of your stomach when something just seems a little bit peculiar? That small voice inside of you that through the course of a lifetime you are conditioned to ignore? I blew it off. I now know that the Holy Spirit speaks to me in this way: a small voice inside of me whispering words of warning. I ignored the message.

I was in the living room when he shouted to me from his office in the back of the house. I heard him say something about insurance, but I could not understand exactly what. He had provided health and life insurance for our family through his business, and I knew that this was one of the issues I needed to discuss with him. My husband had sold him the policies when he was working for the large insurance company before taking over the running of this man's oil business.

I did hear him asking me back to his office.

As I walked through the kitchen to where he was, just as I rounded the corner, he pinned me against the wall. I was blindsided. I was terrified. He began rambling on about things that frightened me. He was saying things about how he had a million-dollar life insurance policy on my husband and that he knew that we also had taken out a rather large policy. I heard something about having my husband eliminated. I started to cry. He said that he knew that the woman my husband had run away with was loaded. He said her father was loaded. He said that her father would do practically anything to avoid a scandal. He lay out in intricate detail how he could carry out the deed of having my husband eliminated. He stated that I could cash in on our insurance policy and together we could extort even more money from the woman's father. He then said that he would take care of me and the girls the rest of our lives.

I began blabbering bits of sentences. I said that he didn't have to take care of me or the girls. I said that all I needed was for him to keep us on his health insurance until I could secure a job. I didn't get it.

His mouth twisted into a smirk. His eyes became dark and narrowed. He said, "You don't understand. I'll take care of you." He tried to kiss me. His grip on my shoulders became painful. All I could answer was, "I want my Daddy!" I broke free of his grip and ran as fast as I could through the hallway, across the living room, out the front door to my car. I was shaking all over. I was sobbing into my hands as I leaned my head against the steering wheel. After a moment, I started my car and sped away. I remember driving and driving and driving, headed where, I had no idea. I thought of running to my father, but I was afraid that he would head straight for the man's home. I did not trust what that evil man who had just forced himself on me would do to my father. I knew he had guns. I knew now that all the stories I had heard about him were true.

My thoughts turned to the man's wife. I was supposed to have lunch with her. I couldn't face her. I never wanted to see either of them again. I wondered how many times he had done this horrible thing to her. I was in a daze. I went to a friend's house. She and her husband had been my confidants during this crisis. I had to tell someone. I was terrified. How much more could I stand?

My friends listened intently. They were not surprised by what I had just endured. They knew of this man's reputation. They warned me that he had dangerous connections and to be very careful.

For days I was living in a dreamlike state. One day I received a phone call. It was the man. He didn't let me say hello. immediately as I answered the phone, he said that his wife wanted to know why I had not waited for her that day. She had questioned him. She asked him if he had done something to me. Then the threats began. He said that I had better never say anything to his wife about our "conversation" that day.... or else what he had described about eliminating my husband would happen to me. This man had connections all over the world. I knew he could make good his threat. I kept quiet. The bad dream I had been living was fast becoming a nightmare.

My days were filled with visits to my lawyer and trying to sort out the financial mess. We had, only a few months earlier, purchased the massive home I was now living in with my daughters, and still had not sold the old farmhouse we had moved out of. The bills were mounting. I had no money and no income. I couldn't sell either of the houses because my husband's name was on the deeds. My lawyer had instructed me that I was going to have to begin the process to have my husband declared legally dead so that I could sell the houses and the vehicles.

It was my thirty-second birthday, May 25, 1984. My father and step-mother were going to take us all out for dinner. Until this day, my daughters had managed to survive all of the chaos which our lives had become. To this point, they only knew that their daddy was not home. My seven- and eight-year-old daughters never asked why or where he had gone. They both seemed to want to pretend that nothing was wrong. That was about to change.

I was standing in the shower getting ready for my birthday dinner when all of a sudden the shower door was flung open. Both of my daughters, fully dressed, ran to me, clutching at my legs, crying hysterically. I tried to calm them down. They bolted from my arms. My

Oldest ran to her room while the younger one curled up in a ball beneath my dressing table. They obviously had faced the fact that something was wrong, horribly wrong. I had to tell them, but tell them what? I myself didn't know what was going on. I only knew of the "woman in Texas" from the story the oilman had told me. I did not know where their father was. I called my father. He and my step-mother came immediately. The three of us managed to calm the girls, dry them off, and get them ready to go to dinner.

Upon our return from the rather somber birthday celebration, I put the girls to bed and joined my parents in the living room. I became enraged. I had endured enough. I had to lash out. I went to the closet where I kept our photo albums. I retrieved the box containing 187 slides of our wedding. Despite the fact that it was a rather warm May evening, I grabbed two huge logs and set about constructing a raging fire. As I tossed each of the slides into the flames, my thoughts raced back to our wedding day and the unity candle. My mind then propelled forward to the day of the explosion and fire. Was I responsible for all of these horrific scenes? Was this again my punishment for standing at God's altar and reciting vows of till death do you part to a man I loathed?

I felt that I was being punished, and now my girls were being punished. How appropriate that scenes from our wedding day were now being reduced to ashes in front of me in a pit of fire. There it was, staring me in the face. I had allowed the snake Satan access to my life through the open door of lies. I might as well have been Cleopatra grasping the asp and placing it next to her heart.

The next morning, I began sorting through the mounds of bills that had been piling up over the past week, bill upon bill upon bill, every day more reminders of the circumstances I found myself drowning in. As I opened the phone bill, I could feel my heart pounding in my brain. There were phone calls charged to our home phone that I did not recognize, phone calls to Texas.

This was what I had been searching for, a link to where my husband might be. I found the credit-card bill. On it, I discovered charges from a hotel in Houston. The dates of the charges were during the oil show. Why a hotel? During that time, he was supposed to be staying in his boss's Houston mansion, the one on, of all places,"The Street of Dreams". This was the proof I had been searching for. He had taken the woman to a luxury hotel and charged it to our credit card. I grabbed the phone bill, located the Texas prefix, and began dialing the numbers.

The first number rang and rang with no answer. The next number was answered on the second ring. The female voice answered in a distinctly Texas accent. "Hello!" I said my husband's name and asked her if he was there.

She said, "He's at the club, playing golf. Can I give him a message?"

I said, "Yes. When he is done with his golf game, have him call his wife!"

Click, she hung up.

About as long as it takes to finish a round of golf, the phone rang. It was his voice, "What do you want?"

I said, "You in the courtroom Monday morning, or I go on the stand and spill my guts about all of the things you have done." I went on to list: arson, income tax evasion, hiring men to beat someone up. "Should I go on?" I told him of the preliminary divorce hearing and said that he had better make an appearance so that we could begin to settle all of the things necessary for our divorce. He hung up on me.

The next day was Sunday. That afternoon my father phoned. He told me that he had received a call from my husband, who was in town and wanted to talk to me. I said that I wanted nothing to do with seeing him unless it was in the courtroom. My father reasoned with me that I needed to talk with him, that we had quite a few details to be worked out. My father was always the voice of reason. I agreed to meet that evening.

I loathed him. I wanted nothing to do with him, nothing short of slapping him across his face when I laid eyes on him. He was even more disgusting to me than he had ever been. His arrogant posture spoke volumes. His lips began to move, and I think that I almost heard a hissing sound as his deep voice began to speak. Reluctantly I listened as he leaned forward, placing his hand upon his knee, a stance I had seen many times when he was closing in for the kill of a business deal when he wanted to exude sincerity and honesty.

The meaningless words, "I'm sorry," bounced off the walls of my father's tiny apartment. I'm sorry was all he could manage. It was as if he had merely stepped on my toe or something. Sorry, sorry! He went on to propose that he would like to come back home. He said that he would live on the lower level of the house, and the girls and I could live on the upper level. It was as if he was merely planning vacation accommodations.

    I was dumbfounded. I knew in my heart that the only thing he was sorry about was that I had found him. He was afraid—afraid of what I could do to him in a courtroom. His fear felt good to me. I told him in no uncertain terms that there was no chance for our ever being husband and wife again. He had done too much. I could never trust him. I told him that his reputation in our town was ruined. I relayed to him the myriad tales of his dirty business deals I had uncovered. I reminded him of the arson, the income tax evasion. I politely told him that he was finished in our hometown. Everyone knew how he had abandoned his family. I told him that the best thing he could do for himself was to go back to whoever it was on the other end of my Texas phone call and tell her that he had made a mistake by going home. I told him his only future was with her.

    It may take a snake several weeks to shed its skin. It only took a second for this man to completely morph from a posture of repentance back into the arrogant person I had known for the better part of my life. There was no remorse in his bearing. He was just afraid of going to jail.

    The hearing was postponed. He retained a lawyer. Just as a snake will strike only if it feels threatened, from that point forward he coiled himself around his pillar of lies and prepared to mount his attack. The battle over stuff and things began.

    This is the point when I began pulling even further away from the church, retreating into myself and asking

God almost daily, "Why? What next, a plague of locusts?" Words have power. I have learned that what you put into words can actually direct your future. God sent ten plagues down upon Egypt before he sent fiery serpents to the Israelites. I had no knowledge of what it meant to challenge God or what a self-fulfilling prophecy was. Through the next season of my life, I would regret speaking those prophetic words. I was learning the truth of the saying, be careful what you ask for—you just might get it.

I was trying to secure a job, and we had put the new house on the market and unlike our still listed old one, it sold quickly. When we went to the closing at the bank, my lawyer and I were ushered into a huge conference room filled with men in suits seated around an enormous mahogany table. My husband and his lawyer were also present, as was our realtor, a longtime friend who had handled the sale of the home. The banker in charge of the closing began reading the list of all of the various dollar amounts involved in the transaction.

When he read the profit from the sale of the house, the figure was around ten thousand dollars. Then he began deducting from that profit all the mountain of bills that our lawyers had negotiated to be paid from the sale. The balance was eleven dollars and change.

As the banker extended his hand towards me with the check for this meager sum, my husband blurted out, "Where's my half?"

The banker was stunned. Everyone in the room was stunned. Both our lawyers knew that I had not received a penny from my husband the entire time of our separation. He claimed to have no money.

Since this meeting was after 5:00 p.m., the banker said that it was too late to cut another check. He turned to my husband and said, "By all means. Let's make sure that you receive your half." He pulled the money from his own pocket and paid us in cash.

We had another meeting a few days after that, also with our lawyers present. My husband left the meeting first. As the three of us remaining were leaving the building, his lawyer turned to me and asked if he could ask me a personal question. My lawyer gave me a nod meaning that it was OK. The lawyer began with, "I don't want to be rude, but how did you ever get mixed up with such a X#@@@?"

I froze, unable to move. In words audible only to me I heard, "Eyes wide open." I had willingly placed myself into the fire. I knew that when I had vowed to love, honor, and obey a man I detested, I was lying. I chose to lie down with the serpent. As the saying goes, when you lie down with snakes you will eventually get bitten.

In the courtroom, for the final hearing, I so much wished to seek revenge. But that was not for me to do; that would be up to someone else. However, just as I had felt that day when he walked out the door, I felt free at last from his presence in my life.

It would be a short-lived freedom.

# CHAPTER 6

## THE SNAKE PATH

> ...... one of these ways is called the Serpent, as resembling that animal in its narrowness and its perpetual windings....and he that would walk along it must first go on one leg and then on the other; there is also nothing but destruction in case your feet slip, for on each side there is a vastly deep chasm and precipice, sufficient to quell the courage of everybody by the terror it infuses into the mind.
>
> Flavius Josephus, The Wars of the Jews, bk. VII, Ch. 8.

THE DIVORCE FROM my first husband launched my life into a zig-zag pattern like Josephus' Serpent path. It began with a move to Texas to marry my second husband, a quiet man whom I had known for almost ten years. He had moved to Texas several years before to pursue a career with a leading tobacco company. His first marriage had ended due to the infidelity of his first wife, a woman also named Susan.

My two daughters had only met him briefly during a lunch with their father, who had also been his longtime friend.

Over the phone, "long distance" from Texas, he asked me to marry him. We had not so much as gone on a date, yet I decided to pack up my daughters and follow this man, whom they barely knew, to Texas. My close family and friends were quick to throw words of caution, like "rebound" and "It's too soon." I heard them all.

The one phrase I did not hear and probably should have was, "You can't run away from your troubles."

I had been running away from the bad things in my life since I was a little girl. Living with a mother who suffered from extreme mental illness had given me plenty of reasons to flee from the chaos. I remembered as a small child running out the door to get away from the torment of my mother's oppression. Too young to understand what was working in her life, I would escape the only way I knew how—I would run away. I remember one time when, tears clouding my vision, I was about to run into a busy street when I felt the firm hands of my big brother clasp the back of my cotton nightgown and pull me from danger.

I don't know if I was subconsciously running away from the mess that was my life after my divorce, or running to something. Whatever the reason, it was the beginning of my using the phrase, "It must be God's plan." I have learned since, in reality, I was taking each piece of my life, each upheaval or tragedy, and slicing away at the edges in order to make it fit into some master plan of my design, not God's.

Some people call it fate or coincidence when things happen out of the blue and appear to fall into place or make some sort of sense out of the chaos of their lives. I now know that every moment of life is filled with opportunities and choices to make, a choice for what is good in God's eyes. It is what we decide to do with those opportunities, how we respond to the events of our lives, that is important. That free-will thing that God blessed us with comes into play. God does not force us down one path or the other. The path that I chose to travel began with that first move to Texas.

The move to San Antonio, Texas, and the marriage to a man my children barely knew was doomed from the beginning. Our wedding was scheduled for two weeks after our arrival. My future husband purchased a brand new home for us in a good school district. One week before our wedding, his brother, wife, and two sons moved in with us. And then, within two months after the dissolution of my first marriage, I again found myself standing at an altar promising "till death do us part."

My second husband's career called him to move to, of all places, Odessa, Texas. I remember the first time I laid eyes upon this desert city from the window of an airplane. My exact words were, "There must have been a nuclear war we knew nothing about and this was Ground Zero!" I did not know about prophetic words at that time in my life, but prophetic they were. This would eventually become the place where I would do battle with the devil, where the snake would almost devour my life. My personal Ground Zero.

The four years we spent in San Antonio had been the launching pad for my career in the retirement industry. I was able to continue that career in Odessa and West Texas, and it proved to be successful and fulfilling. My marriage, on the other hand, began a downward spiral into constant conflict and quarreling. The girls hated their new surroundings. Although we lived once again in a country-club setting, our lives at home were filled with an ongoing battle between the girls and my husband, which put a further strain on the relationship between us. He had never been around small children, and the girls, of course, still adored their father. Due to the hasty marriage, they had not had time to adjust to this stranger in their midst, whom they saw as not only taking their mother away from them but also trying to replace their father.

The marriage lasted only five years. Although we parted friends, I held inside a deep resentment towards him. Our marriage had been a loveless one for reasons I could not quite understand. Truth be told, I think that we only had sex around ten times in the entire five years. It was only years after our divorce, when I had a conversation with him, that I discovered that the sight of my body, which had obviously born two children, was repulsive to him. It had left him with no desire for me as a woman. Our wedding night had been less than eventful.

He had been adopted as an infant, and his adoptive mother was less than nurturing. Years later after our divorce, he confided in me that it was my gift as a good and caring mother that had attracted me to him. There it was: he had wanted a mother, not a wife. Rejection and embarrassment welled up inside of me.

By the time of my ex-husband's revelation to me, I had already begun my journey into the depths of the world and what it had to offer, including sexual immorality. The day that my second divorce had been final, I remember vividly my first step into my jagged future. I was standing beside the pool of my apartment complex, having just consumed a large quantity of wine. I raised my fist to heaven and with words loud enough to shake the future, I proclaimed, "I'm tired of doing things your way. Where has that gotten me? Now I'm going to do things my way!"

The girls' father was a persistent presence in our lives and the catalyst for constant tension. He had married the woman he had had the affair with within one month of our divorce and had relocated to Houston. The girls' scheduled visits to their father were often punctuated by phone calls to me with the ominous words, "We want to live with Daddy." With each of these calls, my heart was ripped from my chest. I never wanted them to feel like they had to live with me. I wanted them to love and know their father. I wanted them to have the kind of relationship that I had with my father. My mother was constantly trying to destroy that relationship; she would stop at nothing to destroy his place in my heart, a place she desired to own. What I was blind to was the fact that while my girls were living with their father, they were subjected to the results of his increasing alcoholism, a fact that would eventually play a role in a catastrophic event in their lives.

Years later, during my tour of Israel that brought me to the Snake Path on that mountain in Jerusalem, I happened upon a sign which read, "The Snake Gate." When I read those words, a chill ran up my spine because I remembered how events in my past had opened my life up to many things God says to avoid. I remembered how, as a young girl, my best friend and I had played with an Ouija board and how we had accused each other of moving the planchette to spell out a name. At the same moment, we had realized that neither one of us had been moving the piece, yet it was spelling out a name. I also remembered how, on a business trip, I had let someone read my tarot cards and that this woman seemed to know things about me. I had innocently opened the gate to the dark forces of this world and had been a prime candidate for their attack upon my life. When I had raised my fist in defiance at God that night by the pool and made my proclamation to live my life without Him, I had opened up the gate even wider to my journey into darkness.

    Once I had entered through the gate, nothing stopped me. Doors began to open, enticing doors which led to successful worldly careers which included television and huge corporations. I had given myself over to this world. I rarely thought about God. Worse yet, I ceased to pray. Instead of reading the Bible, I focused on other written words, words written by men and women inspired not by God but by the serpent. He is crafty. This became my Cosmo Girl period. If the magazines said that it was OK to do, say, wear, or think, then it was OK by me. This time my choices led me on a crisscross path back to the Midwest. This is the dark time I referred to earlier while I was fighting for my life--the visions of the darkest, lowest point in my life. It's ironic that I refer to it as the lowest point because it was during this time when I was actually living on the 54th floor of a high-rise overlooking the Mississippi River.

On a business trip back to the mid-west I had been reunited with a man I had dated in high school. This unholy union, filled with all that is perverse in a relationship, was like a cancer feeding upon all of the rejection, fear, and confusion I had experienced. I was only 36, but I felt like I had lived a million years on this earth. My daughters had both moved in with their father. I was alone and vulnerable. The boy I had dated in high school had been filled with control and anger issues, the very reason I had ended our relationship the latter part of my senior year. His journey into adulthood had only served to increase those traits and to acquire a few new ones. In my desperate search for belonging, I mistook attraction for love.

I was not an innocent in this equation. My self-image and self-esteem had deteriorated, along with my sense of what is right and wrong. At this point, I was willing to do almost anything in order to obtain what was missing in my life. It was the perfect storm. I was isolated from my family and close friends back in Texas. The lifestyle I began to lead in no way resembled the Christian girl I had been raised to be, I was miserable and alone. I felt as if I had nowhere to run. This time I wished to run away from myself. The parking garage beneath our building became my sanctuary. I would hide out in the back seat of my car, not wanting to go back up to our apartment, although most of the time this was unnecessary because he would stay gone for days. I knew in my innermost being that I had no business in that place, that city nor that lifestyle but still I did not reach out to God. I didn't even know whether he existed anymore.

As bad as my life was, I remember the day when I was glad that I was not the woman on the other end of a phone call. The call came from Houston, and the voice I heard was that of my first husband's second wife. She seemed a bit distraught although she began our conversation in small talk. She remarked that we had never been allowed to talk very often. I explained to her that there was a very good reason that our communication had been held to a minimum over the years because he was afraid that we might begin comparing notes—exactly what was about to happen.

She asked me if I thought that she should be concerned about her safety. I had been aware that she had filed assault charges against her husband and that they were in the process of a divorce. I asked her why she would ask me such a question. She went on to explain that he had been asking her to go to their boat, a yacht which I had visited when picking up the girls, to retrieve all sorts of papers he needed. I did not understand the significance of this statement until she went on to explain that the heating and air- conditioning maintenance man for the boat had called her to inform her that someone had tampered with the heating system and it could explode.

Of course my mind raced back to that July night so many years ago when the small boat in my driveway had exploded before my very eyes. I asked her if she knew about this event, to which she exclaimed, "Oh that horrible accident?" She gasped when I said, "That was no accident. He set that fire." The silence was broken by my next words, "Be afraid. Be very afraid."

Not long after this event I received a second call from Houston, this time from the new woman my ex-husband was now living with. She and her youngest daughter had moved into his home and were now living there along with my two daughters. She had been talking with my oldest daughter about why she would not visit me or even speak with me on the phone. She was calling to tell me that she had persuaded her to make a trip to visit me in St. Louis.

It was on that trip that more lies were exposed. While my daughter and I were traveling back to Missouri from visiting my family in Indiana, she began to lash out at me. It was raining heavily, and we both had become upset, so I pulled over at a rest stop. There, with the rain pounding so hard upon the roof of the car that it almost drowned out her words, I listened as she explained why she had pulled away from me: her father had told her that the reason she suffered from cerebral palsy was that I had not taken care of myself during the pregnancy. The lies and deception had known no boundaries. I gave her the facts of what had actually happened and that after going over all of the medical records of my pregnancy and delivery the doctors had said it was most likely that the injury to her brain occurred when I fell and went into shock the night of the fire.

She began to sob uncontrollably. There in the rain, on the side of the highway we held on to each other and cried. The truth had been revealed. A look of understanding and forgiveness spread across her face. A look I will never forget. The years we had been separated by a lie had vanished in an instant.

Satan's reign of terror to control the lives of me and my daughters was not over. About a year later another phone call from Houston precipitated the next leg of my crooked journey. This time it was the assistant administrator from my oldest daughter's high school. She warned me that I needed to remove my daughters from their father. She said that she and others were afraid for their welfare. As she recounted the specific details which were cause for her concern, it was as if I was listening to words which were meant for someone else's ears. She couldn't have possibly meant that my daughters were in danger. But it was true. I had been deceived into believing the lies of the enemy, that I was not fit to be a mother and that my children were better off living in comfort with their father and yet another woman he had recently married, than they could ever be with me.

The woman assured me that she would assist me in any way she could to make the move to Houston to rescue my daughters. She suggested I find an apartment as close to my daughters as I could afford.

As I hung up the phone, the reality of what she had said began to sink in. I waited until that evening to call my oldest daughter to confirm what I had been told. She said it was all true, and I knew I needed to move. I was needed by my daughters.

It was the dead of winter. My oldest daughter was scheduled to graduate that May. I had a developed a timeline that required making some major life changes. I don't know what would have become of me had I not been jolted by my daughters' situation to remove myself from the hell I was living in. I moved out of the apartment I had been sharing with the man.

In St. Louis, I had taken a job at a Dillard's department store when the FOX promotion director's position I had moved there for had fallen through. I had needed a job and had thought that working retail would get me through until I found a job in my field. The "getting me through position" lasted for almost 4 years. I had befriended the woman who had taken a chance and hired me for a sales position against her better judgement. She in fact told me that she knew that I was overqualified for this entry level position but was willing to take a chance on me. Ironically her name was the same as my oldest daughter. When I went to her explaining my need to move to Houston, she arranged for me to secure a transfer to the Houston Galleria store, but I would have to pay my own moving expenses. I moved out of the high-rise and set up housekeeping in a tiny efficiency apartment in the same complex where my boss shared an apartment with another of her employees. Both of these women had become my friends: I was not alone. I proceeded to work extra jobs as a make-up artist to save up for the move.

In May, just in time for Mother's Day and my daughter's graduation, I arrived back in Texas. Joining me at her graduation ceremony was the woman who had orchestrated the reunion between me and my daughter. As we sat together, she began to explain to me why she and her daughter had moved away from my girl's father; her daughter had become so afraid of him that she had begun biting her lip. The woman said that she had witnessed him knock my oldest daughter down the stairs.

My ex-husband and his new wife were seated several rows behind us. I glanced back to see him glaring at the two of us. I'm sure he was wondering what we were talking about. I'm almost positive he knew.

The day after she graduated, she moved in with me under police-protection. She was afraid to move out of her house without a police officer standing by on the premises to protect her from any possible retribution from her father. My youngest daughter, against my advice, wished to remain with her father so that she wouldn't have to transfer schools, a decision which would haunt both her and me because within a few months, he focused his anger upon her.

The police were called to their home. The responding officer remarked that something finally had to be done—they had been called to that address far too many times. Abuse charges were filed. That day she moved in with us.

My oldest daughter had lived under such control that she had not been allowed to obtain a driver's license. Now, away from that control, she began to blossom. Not only did she begin to drive, she enrolled in the local community college and secured her first job.

Life in our tiny apartment was not easy. The girls were in constant conflict. I was now their sole support and needed to increase my income. I managed to secure a job with an international cosmetic company called LaPrairie, which provided a much-needed salary increase but also required me to travel extensively. My youngest was involved in athletics, and my oldest was in the middle of a long-term relationship. I was rarely home, and neither were they.

During preparation for the abuse trial, my ex-husband's attorney coached him that it would look better if one of the girls were living with him when the court date rolled around. He began to approach our oldest with promises of a new vehicle and how things would be different if she returned to live with him. She finally had received the attention she so craved from him. She moved back.

The time of the trial was approaching. I had been subpoenaed by the district attorney to provide him with testimony about my experiences with my ex-husband. He began to read to me file after file of women who had experienced abuse from my ex. He asked me if I had ever experienced violence at his hands to which I recounted one instance which occurred shortly after the birth of my second daughter. It happened one evening after leaving a Christmas party. He was at the wheel of the car drunk as usual and had run the car off the road. I managed to remove him from behind the steering-wheel of the car and drove the rest of the way home. It was necessary for me to help him into the house where he immediately became sick. As I was attempting to help him, he became enraged and took a swing at my face though not making contact. The only contact occurred when his head slammed the porcelain commode as I shoved him to the ground. He was out cold the rest of the night. The recounting of this scenario brought a smile and a, "Wish more women did that," response from the D.A.

My daughter had hoped during the abuse trial that her father would apologize to her for what had happened. That was not to be. She had opted to be present in the courtroom when the verdict was read. He was merely given deferred adjudication and probation. She received no apology that day, only an arrogant smirk as her father passed her by on his way out of the courtroom.

My career was beginning to take off, and so was my continued journey into worldliness. The sirens' song of glamour and success lured me even deeper into a path of sin. Sak's Fifth Avenue and Neiman Marcus were two of my accounts. I was on the outside looking in at the lifestyle of the rich and famous. The possibility that one day I could be one of them was constantly dangling before me like a carrot before a horse. All restrictions are off in that world. If it feels good, you can do it. The gate had already been opened, and it was all too easy to continue down the enticing path.

One day as I was helping a Neiman's employee ring up a $2,000 sale, I heard a voice.

"What are you doing? There are people starving in the world and you just helped a woman spend $2,000 on junk to make her feel better about her outside self."

Where in the world did that come from? I had never experienced such a thing. I was bewildered, yet somehow I knew that the words came from deep inside of me, from some forgotten, distant self. I returned to the present, to the world. I was good at the world. I was good at my job, so good that the Dillard's corporation approached me to return to them. They had been monitoring my success with LaPrairie and wanted me to produce a sales training program for them. They put the company's private jet at my disposal. I had arrived.

It was during one of the trips on this luxury plane that I realized that God had been watching me, too. As I was looking out over the wing of the aircraft through the tiny oval window, I heard a voice in my head ask, "What are you doing in my sky? Your life is in the gutter, yet here you are up here in my sky!"

He had seen it all—the men, the madness, the world filled with sex, drugs, and rock and roll. Tears began to flow down my professionally made-up face, but I shook off the words as easily as you shake off a fly buzzing circles around your head. Back to reality, back to the real world. That is where I belong, down there.

A few weeks later, as I was driving late at night from Baton Rouge to New Orleans on one of my monthly trips, I turned on the radio to keep from falling asleep. A hellfire-and-brimstone preacher who sounded like James Brown in distress was railing on and on about Jesus. The noises he emitted in between each "Jesus" were unintelligible. But the voice I heard was very distinct.

"What do you think you are doing? This car could easily slide off into one of these bayous and leave not a trace. They wouldn't even know where to begin looking for you. And for what? The love of money. Your life is nowhere. Your daughters' lives are nowhere. Yet here you are."

Within a few weeks of this last message, I was given another message, this time from the Dillard's management. There was going to be a corporate downsizing, and I would have to decide whether I wanted to move to Little Rock, Phoenix, or Dallas. This time I raised my voice in defiance and said, "Dallas? I'll never live in Dallas!"

I have learned since that day never to say "never" or "always" about almost anything. It has a way of making you out to be a liar every time. This would be true in this case, but not for a few more years. God had another leg of my journey mapped out for me, a journey that would bring me full circle back to Odessa and the plans He had for my life.

    The Snake Path that the passage from Josephus above refers to is located on the eastern ascent of Masada, the ancient fortified temple built for King Herod. It was constructed in a zigzag pattern because otherwise it would be too steep and treacherous to travel.

    The direction of my life beginning with my first move to Texas would soon resemble this ancient path. My journey was winding, with danger waiting each time my foot slipped. The chasms which I fell into were deep in a life of sin and destruction. If I had known the terror of what was waiting for me along this crooked path, perhaps I would have taken a different route. But I didn't. I blindly put one foot precariously in front of the next and tried to keep my balance along a dangerous way.

    The path the snake had enticed me to follow would now lead me to a place where the journey would all make sense, to a place where God would use all of my past mistakes and tragedies for His purposes, a place where I would eventually face my personal Armageddon back in the desert.

# CHAPTER 7

## SNAKE HUNTER

Luke 10:19 NIV

I have given you authority to trample on snakes and scorpions and to overcome all the power of the enemy; nothing will harm you.

I CHOSE TO GO BACK to the desert, to West Texas. I was tired of traveling, tired of staying in four-star hotels but arriving after 10 p.m., waking up before 6 a.m., not knowing where I was till I looked at my Day-Timer. I might as well have been staying at a Motel 6. I still had friends and business contacts in West Texas. I also had kept in touch with a man I had dated while living there, a man I had for a time hoped to marry one day. I was actually on my way to visit him and his family when I received the news of the downsizing.

I learned of an opening at the Dillard's store in Odessa as an area sales manager. I approached the company with a proposal to fill the store-level management position. They accepted my offer and agreed to pay for my moving expenses. My youngest daughter and her new baby, my first precious granddaughter, joined me there. We rented a house which was owned by the man I had dated. He and I began talking about the possibility of marriage.

Two years into this relationship I was involved in a hit-and- run roll-over accident. Miraculously it resulted in a mere trip to the emergency room. During that accident God spoke to me for the third time. As I was hanging upside down suspended by my shoulder harness, He again had said, "What are you doing?" and I had begun to take inventory of my life. I was involved yet again in a sexual relationship outside of marriage. I was still caught up in the world, thinking that it had the answers to the emptiness I still felt. It is a miracle of God that I had survived that accident unscathed. I broke off the relationship that week.

    It was only a few short months later that I met Kent. I had begun attending a small non-denominational church in Odessa, who's pastor had recently performed the marriage ceremony for my daughter and her husband. It was there on a Sunday morning, sitting in the back row of that tiny church with my daughter, her husband and my granddaughter, minding my own business, that I looked up and there he was.

    I don't know what it was that I felt at that moment, although Kent likes to say that it was the sight of him in his Wranglers walking away down the aisle of the church that caught my attention. All I know is that there was something different; he was different. I had made up my mind that I was through chasing after a man. I had vowed to become a single fat and happy grandma. But that was not what God had planned.

I tried to resist the attraction I felt for Kent. He likes to say that he slipped going around the corner and I caught him. All I know is that the more I tried to avoid him, the more God continued to place him before me. From that first encounter, something inside of me knew that he was the one I had been searching for. He was a good, honest, hard-working man. I felt that I did not deserve a man like him although I had been looking for him my whole life, a man like my father. Now here he was, and I felt unworthy. As I like to tell young women, I had kissed way too many frogs and they had never turned into that prince. God had plans for us-- my prince had come.

One of the things I loved about Kent was his dedication to the youth of the church. He had been a youth coach for many years, and like the Pied Piper, young people were drawn to him. I had since left Dillard's and had become the marketing director of a major non-profit agency, which gave me more free time to join Kent as a youth coach at the church. We began to date in September of that same year. I was forty-six, and he was thirty-eight, newly divorced, with two small children, a daughter who was living with her mother and a son, he was raising by himself.

There were too many red flags to mention, but yet it seemed meant to be. We often talked about what we would like to do when we retired, and every time our dreams seem to center on doing something with youth, a camp, or a school maybe. We also talked about our histories.

There was a part of the past my husband knew about. He was all too familiar with the stories surrounding my first marriage, to the father of my two daughters. Kent understood what it felt like to be abandoned with a small child to raise. We had both ignored warning signs in our relationships before we knew each other. My warning signs were a little more obvious than his. I also had given him the details of my second marriage and selected information concerning the two times I had lived with men outside of marriage. It was all of the mess in between those events which I kept hidden. Besides the magazines had espoused the mantra that what happened before your current relationship was your business, just keep it to yourself. Satan loves it when we keep secrets. They become some of his best ammunition.

We were married on March 6,1999, only three days after the birth of my daughters' second little girl, my second precious granddaughter. For the third time I had assumed the role of wife only this time it came with the new designation of step-mother. A few years later, my sweet step-daughter moved in with us and life was good.

It's funny the things people offhandedly say that end up resonating years down the road. One of the women I worked with at the non-profit, had asked Kent if he thought that he could keep up with me. I was well known for my Tasmanian devil whirlwind style of management, always in a hurry, working at breakneck speed, and mumbling something about killin' snakes as I went. Kent laughed it off in his slow West Texas drawl and replied, "Oh, I think I'll be able to keep up with her."

The future would hold a time when this phrase would bring a smile to both of our faces. It would pop up in a conversation at the beginning of our journey into a dark and frightening night. There in the desert, the light in our lives began to fade.

I left the non-profit to assume the position as director of the Odessa Rape Crisis Center. Not long after it was evident that there were more issues which were in need of intervention than just the one issue of sexual assault. The board of the center quickly responded to the need, and the Rape Crisis Center became The Crisis Center, where we responded, along with law enforcement, to any crime where there was a victim or survivors. When 911 was called, 911 called us. We played a role in the training of the local sheriff's department and the city police academy.

I was not content merely to serve as the director of the Center, I felt compelled to take my monthly turn carrying the crisis pager and responding at all hours to the worst-of- the- worst atrocities Satan could unleash. I had become a snake hunter going out in the dead of night seeking to exterminate Satan and his handiwork anywhere I could find him. No longer was I going to sit back and let him attempt to destroy me or anybody else I knew. At times I would be up all night answering call after call and still take my place in the office at 8 a.m. to continue to oversee the center.

After years of responding to calls from victims of domestic- violence situations to which our only answer was offering a shelter program fifteen miles away in Midland, it became unbearable to have the victims balk at this prospect of giving up their jobs, pulling their children out of school, and moving to another city. After much prayer and planning, we decided to open our own shelter in Odessa.

I took on this venture as if it were my own personal crusade. I had lived under the dominating control of a partner. I had been abandoned by a husband. My children had suffered at the hands of their father. While on a crisis call for the Center I had held the hand of a woman as her cuts and bruises were attended to by a nurse in the emergency room. I had seen the look in her eyes when she realized that her only option was to return to her abuser.

I had sat outside of the house for over eighteen hours tending to the family of a woman who had been stabbed to death with a screwdriver by her boyfriend who was angry because she would not marry him so that he could become a citizen. I had gone in the dark that night with her mother and a police officer to where they thought the murderer of her daughter had gone, the officer, gun in hand, and me holding onto the mother with one hand and a flashlight in the other. He was not there.

One of the detectives and a Texas Ranger apprehended the murderer at the bus station in Lubbock later that night. I had comforted the detectives as they emerged from the house with a look on their faces I will never forget; these seasoned officers had seen it all, but not this. They had watched rescue personnel use the jaws of life to pry the woman's body from beneath the floorboards of a closet in her bedroom. I had accompanied the woman's mother as she walked to the ambulance to identify her daughter's body.

I wanted all of the men who had cursed, threatened, and refused to open the way for creating a shelter in Odessa to be standing beside me right there witnessing the same nightmare I had for the past eighteen hours. I wanted them to feel the helplessness their victims had endured.

The memories of all of the carnage I had seen while at the Crisis Center came flooding back to me. I had held down an eighteen-month-old little girl while she suffered through a sexual- assault exam, knowing that I had written the grant that acquired the machine which was now hurting her as it was painfully gathering evidence from her tiny body.

I began to remember all of the men and women who had ever hurt me in my life. I had seen enough. I had lived enough. I had had enough. It was as if all the anger I had stuffed down inside of me for the past 50 years of my life came bubbling up to the surface. I was angry at the world who had created all of this mess. I was angry at God for allowing all of these things to happen. I was tired of cleaning up after Satan's battles of power and control over the lives of women, children, and families. I was on a crusade, and anger and revenge were my fuel. I did not realize that I had taken the first step towards my own destruction. Anger, hatred, and revenge became the perfect venom which Satan would use against me.

I was unaware at the time that deep down inside I felt that opening the shelter was the way I was going to redeem the twenty years I had lived away from God seeking the world. My conscious mind could only focus on the crusade in front of me.

I had tried all that I knew how to raise money to build the shelter. I had gone before the city council two times to no avail. The non-profit I had formerly worked for, one of our major funding sources, I believed, was playing some sort of political game and had withheld their support of the shelter project. The key phrase I used was,"I, *had tried.*"

Harold, the president of the Crisis Center's board of directors was a captain with the Odessa Police Department and was randomly assigned to be the liaison for Governor Rick Perry's upcoming visit to Odessa and would accompany him in his car during the visit. I used the word "randomly," but there was nothing random about it. What I had been unable to accomplish, God was about to do. While alone in the car that day with Governor Perry, Harold told him the story of our struggle to open the shelter. Governor Perry listened as he was informed that all of the state and federal money designated for domestic- violence intervention in our area was going to a shelter fifteen miles away and that the victims in Odessa were in desperate need of a shelter and recovery programs in their own city.

The governor not only listened but also acted. He gave instructions for a grant to be written to his office and one to the state attorney general's office to access Violence Against Women Act and Victims of Crime Act funds, money that was provided both by the state and federal governments. I wrote the grants, which resulted in Governor Perry's office awarding us $150,000 while State Attorney General John Cornyn's office awarded us $250,000.

We opened Angel House the week of September 11, 2001. Mrs. Anita Perry, the governor's wife was present to cut the ribbon to open Angel House. Also in attendance were many of the men and women who had stood in the way of the establishment of the shelter. As soon as the ceremony ended, we hurriedly ushered out all of the honored guests because our first resident, a victim of domestic abuse, was waiting for us to pick her up at the police station.

Later that year I was summoned to be present at the annual meeting of the non-profit I had worked for. There in front of hundreds of leaders of the community, I was presented with a plaque in honor of my efforts to open the shelter, presented by the very man who had threatened me on the phone to stay out of this shelter thing, that it was none of my d@#* business. The anger inside of me intensified. I wanted to commit an act of violence right then and there in front of all those witnesses. I wanted to take the plaque and hit this man on the head with it. Ironic that I wished to use violence in answer to what I felt was a personal wrong, the very thing which I had been crusading against. But I held it inside, just as I had done my entire life. I held it inside just until I returned to my office, where I ceremonially tossed the plaque into the trash where I felt it belonged.

It was only a few years after this day when the darkness began to inch its way into my life. All of the sordid details of the cases I had worked personally, as well as those I had learned of through my staff, began to press in on me. The details were too close to some of my personal experiences. Some of the details would serve to uncover the past offenses I had endured; the details I had stuffed deep down inside my memory. The darkness came--the serpent's attack literally came in the night.

# CHAPTER 8

## THE VENOMOUS SERPENT

Deuteronomy 32:24 NIV

> I will send wasting famine against them, consuming pestilence and deadly plague; I will send against them the fangs of wild beasts, the venom of vipers that glide in the dust

SATAN DOES HIS BEST WORK in the absence of light. Most desert snakes prefer to hunt at night versus the heat of the day. If they do venture out in daylight, they prefer to hide away in a dark cool place.

I had faced the Leviathan spirit the night of the fire, now I was about to uncover Python. In an article in by Jennifer Leclaire featured in Charisma Magazine she states that the name Python is derived from the story in Acts 16:16 when Paul encounters a girl possessed with a spirit of divination. The word divination in this verse comes from the Greek word for puthon, which translates in English as "python." *Vine's Dictionary* explains how Greek mythology believed the Pythian serpent guarded the oracle of Delphi until Apollo slew it (and then took on the name Pythian). The word was later applied to diviners or soothsayers, inspired by Apollo.

I would soon discover that this spirit, one of the spirits of infirmity, attempts to steal the calling God has on your life through unexplainable accidents or mysterious illnesses for which there seems to be no cause or answer. He tries to get between you and the Holy Spirit to steal not only your joy but squeeze the very breath of life from you. He desires to take away your ability to pray.

I was about to face Python in all his fury.

He came hunting for me at night, in the desert of West Texas, in the darkness of my bedroom. I did not see him coming. I was sound asleep one moment, and in the next I found myself lying on the cold hardwood floor beside my bed. Confused, I tried to figure out what was happening, how I had come to be on the floor, why could I not focus my eyes. The room was spinning around me. I tried to think. Why did I feel like I was drunk? I had not had anything to drink the night before. What was happening to me? I managed to crawl back into bed. I lay there in silence, trying to regain my senses. I reached out my left hand, searching in the darkness to touch Kent's arm, seeking reassurance that I was not dreaming. Thank God, he was there, lying next to me, the sound of his rhythmic snoring an indication that he was unaware of what had just transpired not five feet from where he lay. Both of us were totally oblivious that this middle-of-the-night event would soon transform our lives into a waking nightmare.

The room finally stopped swirling around me and I was able to fall back to sleep. When I awoke that morning, I reacted with my usual immediate launch from the bed as if responding to a starter's pistol, ready to face the day. I had things to do; I had a crisis center to run, I was on a mission. Instead of rising to attack the day, I found myself face down on the floor. This seemed familiar-- oh yes, last night, or was it this morning? Or was it a dream? Again the spinning room.

Once again in confusion, I struggled to climb back to the safety of our bed and called out to Kent. I remember laughing and telling him that it felt like I had a hangover, a description which was virtually lost on him since he did not nor had he ever partaken of alcohol except the thimble-sized taste he sampled with a few of his high- school buddies (he knew then and there that it was not for him, a decision colored by his knowledge of a distant family history of alcohol related illness). I have always admired his wisdom and resolve on this issue, my delight in his decision being colored by my first husband's alcoholism.

I called into the office-- there was no way that I could work that day. The staff of thirty, the numerous grants, the finances, the volunteers, the thirty-six women and children, the rape victims, the details, all the details, I had to take care of the details. How would it all get done if I was not there to make sure it all got done?

I did not know that this moment, this early- morning incident, would be the beginning of six years of a physical, mental and spiritual attack upon me, my marriage, and my family, an attack which could only have been instigated by the enemy of this earth, Satan the serpent; Satan the Snake.

The whirling dizziness did not go away. For two days the spinning room, the inability to focus my eyes, the debilitating nausea, and the pressure of work--all were still there. I sought a doctor's diagnosis.

I should point out that this was not my first experience with the medical community. Hospitals, doctors, and endless testing had been an all-too-frequent visitor in my life. Persistent blinding migraines during my teens and twenties required hospitalizations. A critical pregnancy had required numerous hospitalizations. A botched hysterectomy had required a transfusion and a lengthy hospital stay. A kidney stone had required surgery the first of two automobile accidents had required two years of frequent hospital stays and excruciating pain. A surgical procedure called a fundoplication had been necessary to remedy pre-cancerous lesions in my esophagus.

By the hand of God, I had weathered the storms of; a mentally abusive mother; the tragic fire; abuse and abandonment by my first husband; divorce; self-destructive and abusive relationships. It seems that Satan the snake had injected his venom-filled devices, pitfalls, and snares into my life at every turn. Almost every conceivable assault or temptation had been launched against my life--yet I had survived. When I was in the midst of the struggle, I had no idea that God would eventually transform my survival skills, learned through these events, into tools of testimony for His purpose and glory.

My first call for answers to this debilitating condition was to my General Practitioner (G.P.), a woman I had known professionally and personally for over twenty years. She and I had been nominated for the local county hospital's Spirit of Woman award in its inaugural year. She had helped many times in my life with various health issues. I had no idea at the time that she would be an integral player in my eventual rescue from this six-year journey into physical and mental madness.

My condition at this time was puzzling to her, so she referred me to a series of specialists.

The first specialist I saw diagnosed me with severe vertigo. For days I was unable to function. Medication eased the symptoms enough so that I was able to return to my work at the center—at least for a few weeks.

One morning not too long after the initial attack, I woke up and as usual attempted to stand, my right foot gave way. I reached out and caught hold of the bedside table, steadied myself, and tried to walk. My right foot just wouldn't co-operate. I managed to limp from the bed to the bathroom. This limp would become my constant companion for the next few months. I was able to get around with the use of a sort-of cane. Kent, ever the resourceful husband provided me with a useful tool to navigate my travels through our house, his nine iron. On the third day, I had had enough; nine iron in hand, I again made a visit to my G.P., which in turn led to the first in a series of tests which would increase in frequency and severity over the coming months and years.

I struggled for weeks, being bounced from one specialist to another, but the doctors could find no reason for my condition. Scary words like "multiple sclerosis" were being discussed. My menagerie of medications was slowly building, medications which began to dull my senses numbing me to what was going on around me, both mentally and physically. Worse yet I was spiritually numb to what was happening in my home and to my family. Satan was launching his attack with a vengeance.

Suspected stroke was ruled out, and a rather aptly named diagnosis of "foot drop" was written into my already burgeoning medical record. I managed to limp through and struggle to attempt to work. Kent's trusty nine iron was unceremoniously replaced with a walker, albeit a tastefully decorated one compliments of my second daughter. I struggled along in this manner for several weeks. The ability to maneuver and maintain the fast pace required to run a growing non-profit was beginning to take its toll. It became difficult for me to make it through an entire day, and my work at the shelter was suffering. I was not focused. I let the deadline for the submission of a grant essential to the financial health of the center, lapse. I was drowning. But more was coming.

Satan came at me a third time in this new campaign of his. The sound of my telephone ringing roused me from a sound sleep. When I answered, the caller asked if I was OK. I couldn't figure out why they were asking me that question. I had not realized that my speech was halting and broken. I could not speak without stuttering.

I had always been able to use my ability to speak well in my various vocations. I was an accomplished speaker. I had given speeches and presentations to thousands of people in my career. I had anchored a television news program in the 80s. I had been a trainer for the Dillard's Corporation, flying throughout Texas, Louisiana, and New Mexico on their corporate jet, using my speaking ability to motivate their salespeople. In my work at the shelter, my voice had been one of my greatest weapons in the war against abuse. It was a loud don't- back- down voice. My speaking ability was vital to continuing my work.

But now I began to stutter. The words which were in my heart and mind simply would not be released from my tongue without stuttering or stammering. Satan had been successful in halting my trademark capacity to run from one assignment to another at lightning speed by attacking my ability to walk. Now he was trying to take away my voice, the voice that had spoken out against injustice and summoned hundreds to join in so many causes. God's voice inside of me was also being silenced; drowned out by the deafening noise of the enemy.

If you have difficulty walking and you have difficulty speaking, running a staff of thirty, fundraising, and going on crisis calls are not possible. It took all the strength I possessed to call my board president and submit my resignation. I left the center that day to go home to die. I was no longer useful. I no longer had a purpose. At that time, in that dark lonely place, I had no idea that Satan was using his powers to engage me in battle. He was winning one small victory at a time.

No longer could I champion the cause of victims of Satan's vile attacks.

At the Center, I had been ready at a moment's notice to spring into action when I received a call in the middle of the night. Now I could barely walk--forget about springing into anything. I began to feel that I had no purpose. I felt like an observer watching from a distance as my body continued along its frightening path to physical and emotional ruin. I felt beaten. I felt that I had no further usefulness. I came home, closed the door, and began my rapid decline into a pit of oppression. I was fully aware that my body was being attacked by one infirmity after another, but I was completely ignorant that an assault so much deadlier was being launched against my spiritual me. Satan was winning.

I went completely AWOL from the body of Christ and gradually became isolated; a perfect prey. I was alone without any defense, while Satan continued his attacks. His next one, like a venom-spitting cobra, was directed at my spiritual eyes. There is a species of cobra, the black-neck, which has the distinct ability to hit at least one eye of its victim eight out of ten times with the intent of bringing blistering blindness to its victim. The snake Satan had me in his sights and his aim was dead on, as he relentlessly launched attack after attack.

My faith in anything began to diminish with each onslaught. His stinging venom found its mark and blinded me to the light of Jesus. Unlike the cobra whose propensity to sink his fangs into its victim and hang on is a defense mechanism, Satan uses his venomous bite not in an act of defense but with the sole purpose of full destruction. I was not like Paul when the snake fastened itself on his hand and he merely shook it off and did not die from its venom. I was rapidly succumbing to the effects of the serpent's poison. I did not know how to shake it off. I remained in the darkness, repeatedly sticking my hand into the woodpile, unaware that there were more snakes to come.

    The town of Big Spring, Texas, hosts the annual Rattlesnake Roundup, an event replete with everything from a rattlesnake- meat cook-off to displays of every conceivable product which can be produced from every single part of a rattlesnake. Before I had become ill, during my first and last visit to this exhibition, Kent and I took our place in the audience for a demonstration which at the time gave me no particular reason to be impressed. In hindsight what I witnessed that extremely hot desert day inside the metal mini- arena was emblematic of what my existence had now become.

    In the middle of the arena was what resembled a boxing ring except the sides of the ring were solid plexi-glass panels. Inside the ring lay an empty sleeping bag next to a large wooden box. An expert snake handler entered the ring and climbed into the sleeping bag as the announcer explained that this expert had been a victim of numerous snake bites and that under no circumstances were any of the members of the audience to in any way try to repeat this feat themselves. He also informed us that as a precaution, a vial of rattle snake antivenom close-by, in case any of the snakes did what snakes will do---"Bite!"

    As the man became settled into the padded cocoon, his assistant opened the wooden box and with a large hook began to retrieve clumps of squirming, hissing rattlesnakes, gently placing them inside the sleeping bag where the snake handler lay still and motionless. This was repeated until 100 snakes had been transferred.

My life at this point had great similarity to this man in the sleeping bag. As if it wasn't bad enough that the experiences I had survived while at the Center, the horrendous acts of man's inhumanity to man, weren't bad enough I began to heap more and more encounters with the dark-side upon myself. For days on end while I lay in the darkness of my bedroom, I invited the filth of the world into my presence by viewing hour upon hour of TV shows which focused on the very tragedies I had witnessed in real life. Sex-centered crime shows bombarded me with Satan's perverse handiwork. It was as if I wasn't satisfied with the snakes already permeating my thoughts; I was like Oliver Twist asking, "Please, sir, I want some more."

Satan was quick to oblige. With the mere touch of a button, I let the snakes pile up one on top of the other until my thoughts and my life were as crowded with them as that sleeping bag had been full of rattlers. The man in the sleeping bag had emerged unscathed but only after the snakes had first been carefully removed—I was not so skilled.

I did not realize that I had a skilled assistant at the ready who could remove the serpents from my life.

Satan was ready for another round. After church one Sunday, Kent and I made a quick trip to Walmart. We were browsing the aisles when all of a sudden, my bladder released. There I stood, in the middle of

WalMart, urine running like an open faucet down my legs. I was humiliated and scared. I wanted to die. We rushed home. There in my bed, my right hand began to draw up like a claw. It began violent jerking motions. I went to the emergency room. For hours my right hand stiff as stone, continued its banging motion. The ER doctor ordered strong muscle relaxers, more mind-numbing drugs. I began wearing Depends from that day forward, adult diapers which my husband would have to frequently change. It wasn't fair. He was a young man. It wasn't supposed to be this way.

I began seeking answers. I scoured the internet. I would type in the various symptoms I was experiencing, and frightening answers would emerge. I did not seek God first for the answers to my condition; instead, I sought a cure from the world of medicine, much like King Asa in 2 Chronicles 16:12, NIV, "In the thirty-ninth year of his reign, Asa was diseased in his feet, and his disease became severe. Yet even in his disease he did not seek the Lord, but sought help from physicians.

My foot could no longer maintain any semblance of muscle control. I was prescribed the use of a custom, form- fitted plastic brace made from a casting of my foot and calf. The plastic brace was engineered with a spring hinge at the ankle which allowed my foot stay erect and allow me to walk. I was once again able to walk fairly easily, still with the aid of a cane.

I found that high- top tennis shoes worked to help hold the braces securely, so. I began to collect them and soon had a rainbow of colors (you'd be surprised how easy it was to find high- tops in size 11 on the clearance shelves of discount shoe stores).

What had begun as an occasional Google search, or "Doodle" as Kent has nicknamed it, looking for answers to my as yet undiagnosed physical decline, soon become an obsession. I had flown to Houston to visit with doctors there and had traveled to Lubbock to see if I had contracted a rare nerve condition, all to no avail, yet here I was trapped inside a body which was systematically failing me. My days consisted of taking the multitude of medications prescribed by an ever-growing legion of doctors, searching the internet for answers, and watching darkness on TV.

Kent's days consisted of working long hot hours in the dusty blistering West Texas oil fields and at the end of sometimes a twenty- hour day, returning home to take care of a wife who barely resembled the woman he had married only a few years before.

My ability to walk had been attacked. My ability to speak clearly had been damaged. But I was still a living, breathing human being. It was time for the next assault. It now became increasingly difficult to draw each breath. Soon I required the use of external oxygen to breathe. A large oxygen concentrator took up residence in the corner of our tiny bedroom, with tubing that could extend to the far corners of our home. The pythons grip was tightening slowly squeezing the very breath of life from my body. I was supplied with a refillable portable device, which allowed me to leave the house occasionally. Still, I became more and more reclusive.

Although cardiac complications are not prominent features of snake bite, in the case of the Malayan viper, death may occur from a heart attack. The heart attack of my soul occurred December 6, 2006. The serpent who up to this time had focused his attacks upon my body now launched an attack aimed directly at my heart. I am not referring to my physical heart-- that one had already occurred several times, symptoms mimicking a heart attack resulting in three heart catheterizations which ruled out heart disease.

This attack on my heart was the loss of someone I held dear; someone in whom I had placed my trust since the day I was born. The call came.

"Your father is dying, if you want to see him alive you must hurry."

My father the man whom I had referred to as my rock, the man I could always count on, was dying.

The airline arrangements to accommodate my oxygen and wheelchair assistance were made, and I arrived in Indiana the day before my precious Daddy slipped into a coma.

As I entered the room, he turned his head to see me. His face showed no semblance of a smile. He was unable to speak but his eyes spoke volumes. We had always had the ability to connect without words; just a knowing look. As our eyes connected, words were not necessary, he was saying goodbye. He had waited for me. He slipped into a coma that day.

The next day as he was being transported to hospice care, something happened which at first I did not understand. That morning I had learned that my mother and my sister had visited my father in his hospital room. This was disturbing to me because we had instructed the nursing staff that under no circumstances was my mother allowed see him. She was a very troubled woman and their marriage had ended after 30 plus years of a very relationship. I had no idea what had caused my mother to behave the way she did, what had been the impetus for her outbursts of anger and her propensity to stir up trouble. I would soon come face to face with the demon serpent which had enveloped her very being; my first encounter with the snake who was now chasing me.

My father had met and married my step-mother, shortly after the divorce. She was a gentle, kind, Christian woman who had made the last twenty-six years of his life rewarding and peaceful, a stark contrast to the torment of his marriage to my mother.

She had gone ahead to the hospice facility to take care of the required paper work. I stayed behind to accompany my father in the ambulance. I was anxious to spend as much time as I could with him and this last trip would afford me the opportunity to protect him. Something inside of me was cautioning, warning me not to leave him alone. Somehow I knew that my mother was not done with her attempts to intrude upon my father's last dying moments. I had witnessed the lengths to which she would go to harass him. His retreats into the bathroom for a few moments of privacy and solitude were often interrupted by her bursting through the door, pointing her fist in his face and shouting at the top of her lungs. He was held captive, helpless and vulnerable, just as I had been at her hands too many times to count.

The two attendants arrived with the gurney, transferred my father to it and the four of us began the journey to the ambulance which was waiting downstairs outside of the emergency entrance. Again everything seemed to be moving in slow motion, just as it had the night of the fire. We entered the elevator and descended to the first floor, exited then walked several long hallways. As we rounded the corner heading toward the exit, passing by another set of elevators, something caused me to turn and look just as the doors of the elevator were opening.

    There she stood, my mother. She did not look at me or the attendants. She did not look down at my father lying on the gurney. Her eyes seemed to be drawn to something above our heads, the expression on her face was chilling. Her hands were drawn back in a claw-like manner and her gasps of shock had a distinct hissing sound. The elevator doors slowly closed.

I never spoke of this occurrence to anyone at the time. I kept the horror of what I had seen to myself not even remotely aware of what had just happened. Only years later, as I sat at the bedside of my dying father-in-law, Kent's dad, would I understand what had just occurred. I had seen the face of evil as it had been confronted by the Angels which had surrounded my father in his final hours.

    Two years ago Kent's father had just been transferred to hospice where he lay waiting for the nurses to administer pain medication strong enough to relieve the excruciating pain from kidney failure. He had endured weekly dialysis for three long years. After he had been settled, I sat down on the edge of his bed to his left and Kent stood to his right at the foot. All of a sudden his eyes opened wide in amazement, he began to look above my head then Kent's. Next he turned his head sharply to glance above his right shoulder then his left. He was only able to mutter a few words at a time, in a trembling voice he managed to say, "There's four!" I knew that he had seen his Angel's. I asked him, "Are they beautiful Dad?" He broke out in a wide grin, slowly raised his head up and down in agreement and answered, "Yes."

The peaceful look on his face as he closed his eyes, said it all. Within a few hours he was gone. At the moment he went to be with Jesus, Kent looked at me and said with a puzzled tone, "I'm not sad," to which I replied, "How could you be. Your Father lived a good Christian life, he is no longer in pain and his Angels were with him right here in this room. What is there to be sad about?"

It was only then, years later, sitting with Kent's Father, that I knew without a doubt that my Father's Angels had been there with him as he was dying and whatever evil force that had been working in my mother had trembled at the very sight of them.

Later that day, as I was sitting beside my father, in his hospice room, holding his hand, a nurse approached me, walking past my brother and sister, she asked if she could speak with me outside. She very gently let me know that I would have to let my father go. I asked her what she meant, and she explained that my father was holding on to life because I had not told him that it was okay for him to go. I was puzzled and reminded her that my father was in a coma and could not hear me. She touched my shoulder and asked me to trust her on this point. Her next words would prove to be prophetic, she said "He can hear you."

I re-entered the room and took his hand and gently, calmly told him that it was okay to go and be with Jesus. I told him not to worry about me. That I was going to be fine, that it was okay for him to go and be with his mother and his two sisters. Within the hour, as I sat there holding his hand, he slipped away.

I had forgotten that on the night that my first husband's father had died many years earlier, I had made my father promise that he would never leave me. He made that promise to me. My father was a man of his word.

Little did I know that only a few short years from that time I would also find myself in a coma at the point of death, hearing the voice of someone telling me to come back, not to go.

Our Father in Heaven has made that promise to us: "I will never leave you or forsake you." This is a sure and absolute promise we can count on. Earthly fathers do leave their children. Some fathers (and mothers), unfortunately, walk out the door and abandon their children, leaving a catastrophic void in their lives. For those of us blessed enough never to experience this trauma, the moment of abandonment usually comes when our earthly fathers pass through death's door into their home with Jesus.

My rock was gone. For me, at the time my father died, I did not understand that he was never supposed to be the rock and foundation of my life, that this position rightly belonged to Jesus. As a result, this moment was my undoing.

The snake Satan attacks at will and with deadly precision. He knows your Achilles heel. He knows where he can levy the most damage. Satan had thrown every other kind of venomous dart at me, and I suppose that he was getting tired of watching me survive his physical assaults. Now he had hit me at my foundation.

My foundation, my life was not planted in a relationship with my Heavenly Father. My foundation was rooted in my relationship with my earthly father. Take away her foundation and she will fall, he must have thought--and fall I did. I wished that they had placed me in a coffin and buried me right beside my father.

It happened while I was there in Indiana grieving. Another part of my physical body received a strike. My left foot was down just as the right one before. I sought the aid of a clinic in my hometown to produce a mirror of the brace I wore on my right leg. I returned to my home, now wearing two braces to walk and wishing that I had died there in Indiana, the place where I had entered into this world.

I began suffering severe chest pains. I underwent another heart catheterization. My heart checked out fine, that is, physically, but emotionally my heart was broken. More importantly, my spirit was broken. The sad and frightening thing is that I wasn't even aware that I had a spirit to be broken. I was completely ignorant of the workings of Satan and his power to destroy, but most importantly, I was completely ignorant of the Holy Spirit and His power to fill me with His healing touch.

I don't remember when the first incident of the painful muscle spasms occurred, but I do remember that the bouts of temporary paralysis were becoming more frequent. With absolutely no warning, I would be stricken with intense muscle spasms that would contort various parts of my body into the strangest positions. Often, the attacks were focused on my right arm and leg. I could be resting quietly or engaged in a conversation-- it did not seem to matter. At times the symptoms would begin with the right side of my body contorting, twisting my leg or arm. When the spasms hit both my arm and my leg at once, my body twisted into a grotesque pretzel shape. Often one side of my face would be drawn into a distorted spasm, causing me to look like a disfigured Halloween mask.

At first, these attacks lasted only a few minutes to an hour, but the progression was swift and painful. Oral pain medication and muscle relaxers were of no use. Calls to 911 and trips to the emergency room for injections of Tramadol were occurring almost monthly, often resulting in hospitalization.

The paramedics who routinely answered the calls were accustomed to my condition. There was one occasion in particular that became the impetus for the mantra that carried Kent and me through this frightening time. It was late in the evening when, as Kent used to call it, "I locked up."

Our home was built in the 1950s with rather narrow hallways. On this occasion, my body resembled one of the women in a Picasso painting, you know the ones I mean where the arms, legs, and head of the woman look like they have been processed in a blender?

It was obvious that a stretcher would not be able to navigate the tight confines leading to our room. In his rather pronounced West Texas drawl, Kent asked me, "Do ya' trust me?" Of course, I trusted him. As he placed a blanket on the floor in the same spot where my nightmare had begun, he directed me to put my arms around his neck. As he lifted my, by- then- almost- 200-pound body, onto the blanket below me, he spoke these prophetic words, "We've got to make a decision right now. We either laugh or we cry about this." The decision was evident as the sound of laughter began bouncing off the walls of the tiny bedroom in that small house.

We were still laughing as a rookie paramedic entered the tiled foyer of our home, accompanied by a seasoned veteran, Lonnie, who incidentally was a member of our church. Lonnie had made the trek to our home many times before.

Try to imagine the scene displayed before the novice as he opened the door. First he sees my disjointed body lying on a blanket. Then he sees my husband crouched down on one knee beside me, both of us laughing hysterically. The young EMT obviously did not think that this was funny. To give him credit, he had not been privy to the pact which Kent and I had made just a few moments earlier: we chose to laugh.

His astute observation that it was going to be difficult to place me upon a stretcher was of course not news to Kent, Lonnie, and me. As we frequently say here in Texas, "This was not our first rodeo." The novice declared that he thought that he could straighten me out, and he tried his darnedest to unwrap my contorted body. Our not so quiet chuckles, followed by in unison I-told-you-so's echoed through the house as the two men lifted my contorted body onto the stretcher.

The ability to laugh in the midst of a storm is a gift from God. It can slay the dragons and serpents in your life reducing them to dust beneath your feet. We had learned how to fend off the dragon of hopelessness, if only for a moment. We laughed at the serpent in the storm. We chose to laugh and to love.

As days moved along, I spent even more time at the computer searching for answers to what was happening to me. I would type in all of my symptoms, and a variety of diseases would be presented on the screen. I was tested for all of them. At Vanderbilt University Medical Center, I was poked, prodded, hooked to electrodes, and my hands forced into ice cold water where I had to hold them until I couldn't stand the pain, searching for answers to my illness. There were no medical answers.

There was one possibility left. My search had revealed that there is a rare disorder which affects only 10 % of the population and whose symptoms paralleled mine--- stiff person's syndrome. At the time, the only place where you could be evaluated for this malady was the Mayo Clinic. I immediately made arrangements and flew to their facility in Florida, where I was subjected to various forms of testing. During the final diagnosis meeting, I was informed that there was no finite test for stiff person's syndrome. My test results all seemed to be within the normal range. There were some slight elevations but nothing definitive.

There was an awkward silence so loud that I could barely focus on what the specialist was saying. I vaguely remember hearing him recommend hypnosis. He felt that the source of my illness might be psychological. I was struck by sheer panic. No, no, there wasn't a psychological reason for what was happening to me. I was sick, not crazy--not crazy like my mother, a fear which had gripped me since childhood as a result of living through her numerous psychiatric hospitalizations.

The doctor went on to talk about PTSD (post-traumatic stress disorder). He asked if I had suffered any particularly traumatic occurrences in my life. I laughed. Where should I begin? Being raised by my mentally abusive, mentally disturbed mother? Watching my husband running at me engulfed in flames? The various homicides, suicides, fatality traffic accidents, sexual assaults, and domestic -violence cases which I had witnessed during my tenure as the director of the crisis center? And then there was, of course, this mystifying illness that was wreaking havoc on my physical body. I had been involved in training my staff and volunteers at the Crisis Center about the many facets of PTSD and how to spot the symptoms. I had been schooled by trained professionals on how to respond to victims of a mass critical incident and how to work with PTSD. Of course, I was a victim of PTSD. My whole life had been littered with traumatic episodes.

The doctor proceeded to discuss the procedure for the possible testing through hypnosis. I don't know why, but I was terrified of the thought of being hypnotized. He talked about setting up an appointment for me. I was numb. He gave me a handful of samples of some type of drug. I was given a print-out of the test results.

When I returned home from Florida, I scoured the reports to find some answer that the experts had overlooked. I found one of my blood levels elevated, which happened to be one of the possible markers for stiff person's syndrome. That's all I needed to see. I was not crazy. I was not crazy in the head like my mother. I was not going to end up in a mental institution like she had on so many occasions. I had to have something physically wrong with me. There had to be a name for it. I remember in the midst of this latest onslaught of symptoms, looking to heaven and proclaiming, "What next, Lord? A plague of locusts?" For me, these words became a reality in the sense that every inch of my body was being devoured by infirmity, just as a field of grain can be devastated by a swarm of locusts, like the fields of the family farm in Indiana, where my ancestor had plowed up snakes.

I remember being somewhat confused once, upon traveling to the farm in the fall. The tall stalks that were green in the summer were now a dull crisp dusty brown, all of them still had ears of corn on them. I wondered why they had been left there to wither and die. Why had the corn been planted if it wasn't going to be used? Such a waste, I thought, in my ignorance.

I was unaware that this was seed corn. Seed corn remains on the stalk, and though it appears to be dying, it is drying, awaiting harvest. The huge green and yellow combines which had replaced the monstrous iron, steam- driven threshing machine (still put on display for county fairs) would soon churn up stalks and ears, spewing the separated kernels into the beds of the trucks that followed. Soon the huge silos which dotted the countryside would be filled with the seed corn, allowing it to rest till planting time in the spring.

This is how I felt-- dying on the stalk. At this time, I did not know that I also, was drying on the stalk and that soon the harvester was coming. I did not know that God was about to take my spirit from this dying stalk of a body, hold it for a time and then, after it had rested, remove it from its storage bin and release it back into the fertile fields of His Kingdom. My harvest season was rapidly approaching. My spring planting season was still a long way off.

The next attack was directed at my blood. This one occurred following a particularly severe bout of kidney stones, an affliction which I had suffered throughout my adult life. This time was different. The day after the surgical removal of the stones, I was set to return home. The hospital staff had failed to perform a chest X-ray on me when I was admitted, so before I was discharged I was whisked down to the x-ray dept. The next day, at home, I received a call from my G.P., asking if my husband was home. When I told her that he was at work, she told me to remain calm and to call and have him take me back to the hospital. She went on to say that they had discovered three blood clots in my lungs. My condition was critical.

I returned to the hospital where, by the grace of God, they discovered that all three clots had traveled to locations in my lungs where they could not go any farther. They had been blocked. After a week of painful abdominal injections to dissolve the clots, I was released.

There is a snake known as Russell's pit viper which kills thousands of people every year in Southeast Asia. The venom from this snake causes the victim's blood to clot. I find it interesting that the snake Satan had bombarded me with three potentially fatal blood clots, but God had intervened. Satan wasn't done with me, but neither was God.

 The pain from the ever-increasing spastic attacks became intolerable. The attacks from some family members and so-called friends were just as painful. There are always naysayers who unwittingly become tools for Satan to use in attacks upon your spirit. My skeptics voiced their opinions that I was faking these spasms. On one such occasion, Kent asked a particular critic to tighten his leg as stiff as he could. "See," said the skeptic, "Look it's easy. She's faking." To which Kent replied, "Now hold it that way for 8 hours!" My own family members whispered, "I've seen her walk without her braces. She's faking." It was true that at times the weekly therapy would increase the strength of the muscles in my ankles enough so that I could walk for short periods unaided by the braces. But then it was back to strapping on the knee-high plastic contraptions and stepping into one of the many brightly colored high-top tennis shoes.

 I remember thinking one day as I was completing this ritual that these were the same two feet which had once been adorned with black four- inch high heels clicking through airports all over Texas, Louisiana, and New Mexico. Black designer suits, 4-inch heels, a briefcase and display cases were the standard dress code for executives in the high-end retail cosmetic industry. During an interview with LaPrairie, one of the most exclusive cosmetic companies in the world, I had been asked, "Do you have the wardrobe to dress the part of a representative of our company, the clothes that would work well in Neiman Marcus or Saks Fifth

Avenue.?" I chuckle to myself, if they could only see me now.

Now I sat at home, wearing elastic-waist wind pants ten sizes larger than anything I had worn in those days, lacing up neon- pink Chuck Taylors. The phrase, "You've come a long way, baby!" kept echoing through my brain.

The excruciating pain of the muscle spasms had increased to an intensity which could not be alleviated with oral medication, and the side effects of these drugs were almost as debilitating as the pain. With each new doctor, another mind-numbing medication was prescribed. I now know that I had fallen victim to another of the world's Satan inspired ploys, drugs.

Prescription medication in most cases definitely does work to ease the physical pain caused by sickness and injury, but the effect that has on the brain, the numbing, dumbing down of your mind, inhibits the ability to focus on God and His voice calling out to you. I know this from experience. My typical day consisted of being awakened by my husband with a kiss goodbye and a reminder to take my medications. By this time the total daily count of pills was around forty.

These were not just minor medications. I am talking about Neurontin, Clonazepam, Opana, Lortab, and Miacalcin, and those were merely for the relief of pain and the muscle spasms. Then there were the meds for nerves and depression--, Diazepam, Zoloft, and Prozac. Oh yes, there was that. I would ingest my handful of morning meds and blank out to nothingness, sometimes until 4:00 in the afternoon. So many days stolen from me, so many productive days lost! I often imagine what I could have accomplished for the Kingdom with those lost six years-of-days.

I did not see, I did not even think, that where I should have sought refuge was my Savior. I was blinded just as certainly as if a cobra had spit its powerful venom into my eyes. Satan had ever so quietly slipped his scales one by one over my sightless eyes.

I could no longer bear the pain, and I was referred to a local specialist who recommended that I might find some relief through the use of a pain pump. I was willing to try anything.

The pump the size of a compact disc player was surgically implanted into my abdomen just under the skin. A plastic tube was attached to the pump and then fed under the skin around my left side. From there the tubing continued around my back where it was attached to a catheter which was surgically implanted between two vertebrae in my spine. The reservoir of the pump was filled with morphine. Once a month the reservoir was refilled and a computer pack would be laid against my skin directly over the pump which allowed the doctor to program the desired dosage to be pumped directly into my spinal fluid through the catheter. I received the benefit of the morphine's ability to relieve the pain with none of the mind-numbing side effects.

This method was successful in relieving the pain for only a few months. It was suggested that I needed to have an additional drug called Baclofen mixed with the morphine to ease the pain. The doctor who had implanted the pump was not licensed to administer this combination of drugs so I sought the services of a qualified doctor, who's practice was 15 miles away in Midland. This changing of physicians would prove to be a crucial element in my impending miracle.

I was at that time ingesting 12 oral medications plus the two intra-spinal drugs each day. When I was awake my mind remained clouded in a drug-induced haze. I had become a bitter zombie.

At first, it became difficult for me to swallow, then impossible. I drooled because I could not keep up with eliminating my saliva. I was taken to the hospital. After some testing, it was diagnosed that I was unable to swallow and that I would require the use of a feeding tube. I was taken to surgery where a rubber tube was inserted into my stomach about 6 inches above my navel. I now had to pour liquid nutrients into the tube three times a day in order to live. I died inside a little more.

Eating had become my favorite pastime, my solace, and I indulged in it as often as I could. Now this one pleasure I sought quite frequently to ease the pain and fill the void of my life would also be taken from me. The food which had become my place of refuge and comfort had now been removed from my reach. My taste buds which had once delighted from their penchant for cherry turnovers, ice cream, and my go-to tacos, now were only teased with a hint of second-hand contact vapor with the syrupy flavored liquid feeding supplements which were poured into my feeding tube. It was as if every single source of comfort I had run away to, was being stripped from my life.

Rails were installed on my bed where I spent almost 24 hours a day. The endless days of drugs, TV crime dramas and my new addiction, home shopping network continued to transform me into an unrecognizable shadow of who I had once been. The medical contraptions and the two hundred pounds I now weighed were a far cry from the vibrant, purposeful life I had once lived. I was now completely trapped in a life of prescription drugs, hospitals, and therapies for my legs, therapies to regain my ability to swallow, braces, wheelchairs, hospital rails on my bed, and oxygen tubes to breathe.

One day as Kent was helping me onto the shower chair, he said, as only he would or could, "Still look good in the shower, babe!" Only through the eyes of love could a man look at a 200-pound, scarred body with a skin pouch the size of a compact disc player bulging from her abdomen and a yellow rubber feeding tube dangling from her chest and proclaim those uplifting words. Only a man whose heart was full of the Lord could commit his entire life, his undying devotion with such selfless sacrifice. He had promised for better or worse; this was the "worse" part. We had only experienced two years of the better.

One Sunday Kent convinced me to attend a local church with him. We had ceased making the journey to our home church years before. As Kent was helping me down the aisle to our seat, I heard one of the ushers tell him, "How nice you could bring your mother."

Remember when one of my coworkers asked Kent if he thought he would be able to keep up with me? One day as he was pushing me along in my wheelchair, he teased me, "Yup, I think I'll be able to keep up with her." One of the few things I had been able to salvage from my former self was my talent for sarcasm. Immediately I bantered back at Kent, "Yup, but I'm still ahead of you!" We both laughed.

There were times when he would arrive from work to find me having a rare good day. On those occasions, he would shove the dining room table to the side of the room, roll back the rug, turn on the CD player to one of our favorite country tunes and usher me from the bedroom. As he took me in his arms, we began to "dance." Our stationary swaying to "Waltz across Texas" was nothing like the lively footwork we had executed on the dance floor of the Stardust dance hall the night we fell in love just a few short years ago, although you could not tell from the look on our faces.

Those days were becoming fewer now. Alone in my dark world, I surrendered to what I felt was inevitable. I believed the lie that I indeed did have stiff person's syndrome and the five-year life expectancy was fast approaching. I filed a Do Not Resuscitate order at the hospital where I had been a patient for nearly six years. I made an appointment with a local funeral home and, against the wishes of my family, made arrangements to be cremated. I returned home from this meeting and waited to die.

How appropriate that I should choose a fiery end.

But death did not come, at least not the death I had expected.

# CHAPTER 9

## THE SNAKE PIT REVISITED

Revelation 11:7 King James Version (KJV)

And when they shall have finished their testimony, the beast that ascendeth out of the bottomless pit shall make war against them, and shall overcome them, and kill them.

IN MAY OF 2017, while in the midst of writing this memoir, I was awakened by one of my frequent early-morning appointments with God (it seems that now He likes to give me words at around 3:00 or 4:00 in the morning; I call it GST, God's Standard Time). On this particular occasion, there were only two words that He laid upon my heart, "snake pit." I immediately recalled the classic film of that title, a rerun of which I had watched many years ago. As I googled for background on the movie, I discovered that the 1948 film was based on the 1946 novel by Mary Jane Ward (who like me had been born in Indiana). It tells the story of a woman who finds herself in an insane asylum and cannot remember how she got there. As I recalled the movie, I wished that I could claim to have no memory of how the serpent chose to drag me down into the pit of mental confusion. Unfortunately, I remember all too well the days and weeks leading up to the moments hours and days when Satan the serpent arose from the pit in his most terrifying attempt to claim me.

The pain pump implanted in my abdomen and spine had broken as a result of a fall in my kitchen. Unaware that this had transpired I became increasingly ill for no apparent reason. Due to a break in the catheter the morphine and Baclophen which had once served to give me relief from the pain was now transformed into poison seeping out into my body. My doctor diagnosed the problem and a minor surgical procedure was scheduled to make the repairs. His plan was that I would only remain in hospital overnight following the procedure-certainly not the accidental overdose, the coma, and my encounter with God.

My story has now come to that point where this book began, with my emergence from the coma. I remember thinking that now my life would be different. I had survived all of the past six years and the lifetime before.

While lying in the dark room where they had moved me from intensive care, I was awakened by what at first I assumed was yet another nurse, checking my vital signs. I was mistaken. Standing beside my bed was a tall thin figure, male or female, I was not sure. The figure was wearing white. I remember that this was confusing to me because all of the nurses who had attended to me wore various colored scrubs. I remember shoulder length dark hair with bangs resting just above dark eyebrows. The figure remained perfectly still, stoic, never looking down at me but staring straight ahead as if focused on some point to my left. I remember thinking, why isn't this person taking my temperature or changing my bandage. Why just standing there? Both hands were gently resting on the right side rails of my bed. My gaze was drawn to the left ring finger which bore a simple gold band. As I looked up, I heard these simple words,

"You are going to be OK."

I felt suddenly calm and serene. I closed my eyes and drifted off to sleep. I never saw this figure again. I never told anyone about this appearance until two years ago. During a discussion with a Doctor of Theology, I began to retell the details of this encounter. I asked him what he thought was the significance of the gold band I had fixated on. He explained that very often, a gold band was used in reference to the Holy Spirit.

Could that have been who visited me that day? Right now I don't know for sure, possibly someday I will, what I do know for sure is that from that day forward I was so filled with a renewed spirit that I felt invincible. I had been given a second chance, but the serpent Satan was not finished with me yet. He had saved one final assault, one more strike in his attempt to still my voice. This time he used a weapon I had dreaded my whole life—losing my sanity.

God had healed me from the agonizing pain of the illness. I no longer required the use of the pain pump and desired to have it removed. The pain specialist who had implanted the device in me was not willing to remove it and suggested that my pain doctor who had performed the procedure to repair the pump also perform its removal.

At that time, for fear of administering any type of anesthetic so soon after my emergence from the coma, my pain doctor, the surgeon who had repaired the broken catheter, was able to use only a topical pain medication during the procedure to remove the no longer needed pain pump system. He is from China and loves country music-he especially loves country western dancing, although he claims to have no ability to do the two-step. During the surgery, he had to re-open the incision in my abdomen and remove the pump which now was filled with only saline solution and by this time had become encased in scar tissue. I could feel the sensation of the scalpel cutting and pressure as it reopened the two-year-old incision.

I had requested that they play praise music in the operating room, but that morning they informed me that my request had not been relayed to the technicians. Instead, they were able to tune in the local country station. Familiar tunes began filling the air of the cold antiseptic room.

I recognized the voices of the DJ's as they bantered back and forth between songs. The voices belonged to two of my good friends, Mike and Dana, the morning hosts of the station. They had been a part of my life for many years joining with me in various community projects. The sound of their voices and country music became my personal form of pain relief.

I was busy explaining to the anesthetist that you can take the lyrics of many country songs and convert them to a song of praise to the Lord. He was required to be present to monitor my blood pressure levels. Interrupting me in the middle of my country/praise sermon, he admonished, "Be quiet. I have to watch the monitors."

Once the pump was removed and the incision closed, my surgeon asked me to roll over carefully so that they could begin the delicate task of cutting off the catheter inserted in my spine. It would be too dangerous to totally remove it or the one which was implanted two years ago because the chance of paralysis would be great.

The strain of the procedure began to affect my vital signs. Taking a cue from the music playing, my surgeon devised an ingenious method to help me control my breathing and blood pressure. If my blood pressure was reaching a dangerous high level, he instructed me, "Carol, it's now a waltz." This signaled me to slow my breathing. If my blood pressure dipped dangerously low, he prompted, "Carol, it's now a quick two-step!", prompting me to take deep rapid breaths.

As I was lying face down on the operating table, I began humming to the music and kicking my feet, causing the nurse who was seated at the foot of the operating table to warn, "Be still! He's digging in your spine!" Next, it was time to make a blood-clot patch to seal the interior hole of the catheter to prevent my spinal fluid from escaping. For this task, some of my own blood had to be drawn. The years of IV medications and endless blood tests had left most of my veins too calloused to be penetrated. They attempted to secure the sample from the usual sites in both of my arms with no luck. They next tried to draw a sample from my feet to no avail. Their last resort was to execute a cut-down.

This procedure involves using a scalpel to actually open a vein in the top of my wrist. My left wrist would not give up the required amount. I could see the blood running down over my hand and dripping off my fingers. I knew what was to come. They must now try my right wrist.

I had been praying to God throughout this ordeal. Suddenly I was struck by the vision of what I must look like. There had been punctures made to my feet. I had an incision in my left side, and now there was blood flowing down both my hands. The image of Jesus on the cross began to filter through my thoughts. How He must have suffered when he was crucified! Compared to His pain and anguish, this was child's play.

Finally, they had enough to make the patch, and after a few hours in the recovery room, I was sent home to recuperate.

Back at home, my body was now free from the pump which had at one time filled my body with powerful drugs. Now it was my mind that was being fed an almost daily infusion of random thoughts and messages. I had difficulty understanding and carrying out the simplest instructions. I was like a small child having to learn all over again how to function. I was drowning.

I have researched the effects of a massive overdose of morphine and discovered that there are two options, coma or death. By God's hand I had survived both death and coma. Unfortunately, through either the effects of the drugs pulling poisons out of my system, the coma, or simply the sudden cessation of the fourteen numbing medications I had ingested for six years, my mind was very fragile.

    Most of my recollection of this time, right after I was released from the hospital, is hazy. I remember my husband taking me into the dining room where the computer was. This is where I had spent countless hours working on grants for the center. This is where I had also spent countless hours searching the internet, looking for answers to my medical condition. Now, as he sat me down at that same computer, I had no clue how to operate it. I didn't even know how to turn it on. I held the mouse up in the air--it was a foreign object in my hand. I remember the look on my husband's face, a combination of disbelief, confusion, and exasperation.

    One of the scenes God had played back for me during my encounter with him was of me sitting at that same computer. I could see it all as if it was happening at that very moment, not the six years after its actuality. As I viewed myself from above, I heard my voice shouting harsh words at my husband. We had always teased each other, but this time, during my death experience, I saw how my harsh words affected him. I was mean to him. I was ridiculing him. And I was ashamed. I had been ugly to the man who would, shortly after that incident, love and care for me in a totally selfless way. He loved me in a way few women ever get the chance to be loved. Most couples only get to experience that kind of devotion at the end of a long life together.

    Now here I sat beside him, trying to figure out how to even turn the computer on. I myself was like a computer which had crashed and was taking days and weeks to reboot. When I tried to write, I wrote as I did in kindergarten, with huge block letters taking up six lines on the page. Basic math problems confounded me. I was unable to read; the words made no sense to me.

I now realize just how bewildered and frightened Kent was. My mind was fragile, and my actions bizarre. When I say that I was "born again," I mean it in almost every sense of the word. During the coma and close encounter with death, I had faced up to my sins and had accepted God's forgiveness. I had come out of the coma feeling "born again". I was now not only a Born Again Christian with a never before zeal for a relationship with God, my physical being had also undergone a type of rebirth. I experienced renewed strength in my entire body. Like a master computer expert God had wiped away all the "viruses" which had attacked me for not just the six years of my illness but for decades prior. My many unconfessed sins had been cleared. My slate was clean. However, my battle with the devil serpent was far from over. He steps up his attacks upon us when we are new in the Spirit, when we have heard God's voice and are now a new creation. The devil was angry, and he wanted me back.

All my life, I had been afraid that I would end up just like my mother--in and out of mental institutions, living in the dark. Her mother had lived in mental darkness most of her life: it was a family tradition. With windows covered to keep out the light, my mother had retreated into darkened rooms for days at a time, never allowing in the light, and then into mental hospitals, never facing her demons, trying to hide from them and the world, yet tragically, hiding with them.

To my husband and those who knew me before the onslaught of illnesses, I **was** acting crazy. My mind was so fragile, so new. I was behaving like a newborn child. Everything seemed new and fresh to me. Everything in my world was fascinating. I noticed things as if seeing them for the first time. There were doves flocking to my backyard. I had never noticed them before. My husband told me that they had been coming there for years. How could I have noticed them, shuttered away in my bedroom, wallowing in my despair, my mind numbed by countless drugs? I had shut them out. I had shut everything out. Satan wanted me to die, and I had let him have his way. But now I knew that I was filled with life, filled with joy.

The serpent can numb our spirit with drugs if we let him. If we decide to escape from this insidious hold he has on us, we may face yet another attempt to destroy-withdrawal. The effects of my abrupt dissent into this process were just beginning, effects which became a tool of the enemies plan to destroy me. The powerful drug administered to me that saved my life also left me depleted of the basic minerals necessary for the function of my vital organs. Potassium is vital to your heart's functioning and my potassium level was non-existent. My heart was in crisis. Potassium as well as other vital minerals and metals essential to the brain processes were non-existent. Satan wanted both of these back, my heart and my mind.

I remember bits and pieces of the night it all fell apart. I was sitting cross-legged on the floor in the entry hall of our home. I was crying and rocking back and forth, my fists clutched tightly around a small pillow. I was forcing the pillow against my face. I was trying to do something I wasn't sure of at the time. I only knew that I had a compulsion to cover my face with that pillow. I saw my maternal grandmother do something similar shortly before her death when I visited her in the nursing home. She was lost in another world. She held the edge of her bedsheet clasped tightly in her fists and pulled it up to cover her face. But she wasn't crying; she wasn't fighting whatever it was that was haunting her. She was giving up, quietly surrendering.

I remember looking up from the floor of that entry hall at my son. He was standing over me with a look of sheer disgust. I think that he was telling me something about his observation that this just couldn't go on.

The next thing I remember was standing in my living room. For some reason, my best friend Renee was there. Kent had called her; he was trying everything he knew to help me. He had no clue what was happening to me; he was shell-shocked. I remember how relieved I was to see her. We had been close as sisters for twenty years. We had affectionately labeled ourselves, "Salt and Pepper." She had joined me at the Crisis Center and had assumed the role of Shelter Manager. I had always felt at peace with her. Now, in my moment of crisis, I ran to her and held onto her as tightly as I could. I remember acting in a rather bizarre manner. I remember that I couldn't understand why I was doing these things.

As I was being escorted to the ambulance, the front yard seemed as though it was extremely bright for the middle of the night. Everything was still and silent; it was eerie. It reminded me of the night of the fire when I emerged from house and was faced with the fire.

From here on out and for the next few days, my memory is spotty. I remember being in the emergency room. All of my blood levels were off; I had absolutely no potassium in my system. My mind began to surge out of control. I shouted out the name of my doctor. I was also calling out the name of my first husband. Kent was crushed. Here he was anguished, in a state of utter confusion and exhaustion, and I was calling out the name of my former husband, when it had been he, who had been the one to bathe me, cloth me, feed me and even change my diapers for six years. He asked the ER nurse what was happening. He told him that he had seen this before; sometimes patients pulled out of it; sometimes they were lost forever.

He walked out of the doors of the ER and sat down on the curb and cried--Kent doesn't cry. He thought that he had lost me forever. He couldn't possibly know or understand what was going on inside of me. I was being tormented to the very brink of insanity. He had never known of the promise at the altar and the flames. Somehow it was all tied together. Satan was hitting me with my past, complete with all of my many sins. I wasn't capable of fighting his onslaught of visions and voices.

I had not been taking any medication, nothing after six years of a medicinal buffet of drugs. I was admitted and immediately given IV potassium which retuned my heart-rate to normal; my brain function was still to be repaired. For the days that followed my behavior was bizarre.

I am sure that to the outside world it was crazy; it was crazy to me. I now know that everything I was experiencing was a battle with the serpent-devil. Kent said that I tore the pages out of the Gideon Bible that had been placed in my room. Who but the devil would want me to do that hideous thing? Every muscle in my body was being afflicted with indescribable cramping. I had no magnesium or calcium in my system. My muscles had been starved for nutrients, as had my brain.

I was hospitalized for several days with no improvement. My G.P. was convinced that I was experiencing the effects of withdrawal from years of medication and persuaded the local drug- treatment hospital to admit me until I was stabilized. The administrator was reluctant to take me in because he said that I did not fit the parameters of his patient profile. She convinced him that something unique was happening to me.

My time there was filled with rest, group therapy sessions and playing what seemed to me to be games better suited for children. I felt lost and bewildered. I remember saying that I did not feel ready to leave. I felt as if I needed time to prepare myself to return home. It all seemed to be happening to someone else. I felt a sense of foreboding. After a few weeks I was released back to my home and husband. But something was different. He had changed. He never neglected to see to it that my physical needs were met, but there was a coldness present.

I did not know that while I was in the hospital struggling to get well someone had been using my absence to fill Kent's head full of venom, revealing to him things I had not yet been well enough, not together enough, and not brave enough to tell him, the specifics of things I had kept hidden in my past, all of the sordid details of a life lived in the flesh which God had compelled me to face in my moment of near death.

One evening Kent was called out to work. Afraid to leave me alone in my fragile state, he took me with him. It was during this trip into the blank darkness of the West Texas night that something came over me. I began to spill forth all of the many humiliating secrets that I had kept from him for so long. It was as if I was vomiting the garbage of my life all over the cab of the pick-up. Every molecule of air inside the cab of that truck was filled with the sound of my shame.

He was quiet at first. Then he exploded in a justifiable rage. He shouted at me to stop. He wanted to know why I was telling him all this. He didn't understand. He didn't deserve to hear what I was telling him. I had no way of knowing that he had already been given the sordid highlights by someone I trusted. I provided him with additional details-things no one but God had any way of knowing about, things I had hidden so deep that I myself was shocked to hear them recounted out loud.

I was stripped bare, all of my past finally exposed. I felt as if some force was driving me to reveal these things. I couldn't stop. It was a nightmare. I kept blacking out. I could not control myself.

From that night on and for the next few weeks, my husband was different. There was a distance between us which I had never experienced in our marriage. He had heard from my own lips the things he had been told, only this time I had given him all the details and more, so much more. He was crushed.

My mind was in utter shambles. My memory of the following period of time is spotty. The new medication I was given to make me sleep kept me awake. The medication for the daytime made me sleepy. I remember anger--anger from my husband. I had never felt anger from him before, but he had a right to be angry. I had lied to him, lies which cut to the heart. He didn't look at me the same way. I remember his words. "I can't do crazy. I can handle sickness. I can't do crazy. I won't do crazy."

Was that what I was, crazy? I remember feeling full of the Spirit, but at that time I had no idea of all that those words meant. I was focused on God. I read the Bible with a vengeance. I listened to Christian radio broadcasts. I watched reruns of *Touched by an Angel*, a show I had never watched before. I felt so alive in the Spirit. Music seemed to hold an even greater meaning to me. I listened to Christian music constantly writing down the lyrics in my journal.

Even with the aid of strong medications I couldn't sleep. My body was still racked by horrific muscle spasms, although different and not so severe as before when I was critically ill. I was now using muscles which had not been used in years. I was walking and cleaning house with a vengeance. (My house had not received a thorough cleaning in six years; Kent had done the best he could, but he had had much more to take care of than housekeeping.) The curtains in my bedroom looked like those you would find in a funeral parlor. Barricaded inside a dark and lonely room, I prepared to welcome my death. Now, free from the confines of my bed, braces and pumps, I wanted to clean everything-- my house, my body, my mind, marriage, my entire life.

I felt what I thought was the Holy Spirit everywhere, but did not know how to process all of the sensations I was feeling. My hearing was so acute that, on a visit to my doctor, I was unable to prevent myself from hearing conversations in another room. The receptionist was talking on the phone to a patient. She was separated from the waiting room by a wall with a sliding glass window. I could hear the office assistant talking, that was no great feat. But I could hear very distinctly each and every word that the patient was speaking and I could see that she was not on the speakerphone. I felt as though I were eavesdropping. I tried to block it out by covering my ears, but that did not work. I finally went out into the entryway still covering my ears to block out the noise.

I did not understand what was happening to me. Kent could not understand it, either. He was becoming increasingly exasperated. For six years he had become used to certain aspects of my behavior, but this was all new to him.

The previous year, he traveled with his brother to Montana to participate in a cattle drive. I was so happy that he had taken the time to get away from all of the pressures my illness had caused. It was a dream trip for him. At the end of the drive, he was given the opportunity to schedule a return to the same ranch the following year at a reduced price. He booked his trip for the next August. His sister and brother- in- law had made plans to join them, and it was now time for the trip. I wanted to go with him, but I was in no shape to ride a horse. I would not be able to stay back at the ranch while the drive was taking place, that being against the ranch policy. We decided that I would travel to Dallas and stay with his brother's fiancée while the four of them went on to Montana. That was the plan.

I had quit taking the medication the doctors had prescribed to help with my agitated state because it made me feel worse. I had ingested all of the medication I ever wanted to take. I never wanted to live in a fog ever again. However, the sudden cessation of medication, the depletion of nutrients, and the lack of sleep had begun to take their toll on my nervous system. The charley horses were becoming so intense that at time I was barely able to walk. My G.P. advised me to drink tonic water explaining that the quinine it contained would ease the muscle spasms. It barely seemed to help, I was determined not to resume prescription meds.

I began to feel threatened, by what I could not understand. I felt threatened by Kent. I felt threatened by his brother and was frightened for some unknown reason to be in his home. I wanted to run away. But from what? I wanted to go home. While playing a board game, tensions escalated. I asked that my brother- in- law take me to spend the night at his fiancée's home. All I knew was that I had to leave that house. He agreed to take me to her home, but on the way he became furious and began yelling at me. He couldn't understand why I was afraid of his brother. He wasn't the only one, I couldn't understand why I had this fear festering inside of me.

When I arrived at her home, I felt safe. She and I sat up very late and talked. I told her that I thought that God had a plan for me to complete some sort of mission work. We talked about men and marriage. I slept soundly that night.

The next morning, after she left for work, I roamed around the house and began to fix something to eat. I wanted to go back to Odessa. I wanted to go home. Later that morning, my husband and his brother came over. Kent looked bewildered. He sat on the couch, calmly, and asked me what was going on. I told him that I wanted to go home, that I had called the airline and booked a flight for later that day (I had a credit with the airline and would only have to pay a small difference in fare). He was dumbfounded. He thought that I was leaving him. That was not my intention, I just wanted to go home--I had this fixation that I needed to return home.

Kent had experienced the tragedy of his first wife leaving him, and now, faced with my confusing behavior and his insecurity fueled by the input of outside influences, he told me that if I left and returned to Odessa without him, that it was the end of our marriage. I told him that I did not want a divorce, that he would have to be the one to make that decision.

His brother became enraged and began shouting at me. I was terrified. From that point on my memory is spotty. I don't remember this, but Kent said that I stood up and very calmly stated, "I'm better now. I don't need you anymore."

How could those words have left my lips? How could I have even thought of such a thing to say? This completely shattered Kent. His brother, on the other hand, became even more enraged. He knew how much Kent had sacrificed for me. He wanted to protect his brother. I was frantic. I remember reaching for the phone and dialing 911. My brother-in-law ripped the receiver from my hand. I ran to the bedroom and closed the door. Kent came after me. Years later he told me that he had only wanted to find out what was happening. That is not what I felt that day, I was terrified.

I grabbed the phone in the bedroom and dialed 911 again. Isn't this what I had trained women to do when they were being attacked? But I wasn't being attacked, at least not by my husband or his brother. I was crumbling. My nerves and emotions were shattered. My husband pleaded desperately for me to open the door. When he heard me talking to the 911 dispatcher, he called to his brother. They left.

When the police arrived, I relayed to them the events of the past few minutes. They took me to a shelter. A shelter! It was like a nightmare come to life. Here I was in the back of a police vehicle being transported to a shelter. Everything was in slow motion, just as it had been the night of the fire as if I were watching a movie.

When I arrived at the shelter, I was given a brief tour. It was much larger than Angel House. I was shown to the dining hall and given something to eat. I was in a dream state. This wasn't happening. This wasn't real. Some force outside of me was propelling me into a situation I felt powerless to stop. I called my brother-in-law's fiancée, and she informed me that he had told her that he and my husband were headed to the bank to withdraw all the money, a claim which turned out not to be true. I had heard this scenario played out many times before with the victims I had worked with: the abuser cleans out the bank accounts so the victim will have no resources. The memory of the day I discovered that my first-husband had emptied our accounts and run away replayed in my mind.

    She had misled me. My husband had only gone to the bank to make sure there was enough money for his trip the following day. I took this misinformation and ran with it. Or should I say ran away with it? I panicked, called the airline, and changed my reservation to the next departing flight to Odessa. I had no money on me, and I would need cash to pay for the difference in the cost of the plane ticket. I informed the staff of the shelter of my plans, and they called a taxi for me. I asked the driver to take me to the local branch of my bank, where I apprised them of my situation. All I had was my ID. I had not held a driver's license for several years. I knew from my training that in such cases my particular bank had provisions for someone in my situation to access their bank accounts, even if they did not have all the necessary documentation. I had just enough in my bank account to pay for the taxi, the plane fare, and $20 cash. Everything fell into place. Thank God, I thought, *You are preparing a way*. Or was it another force which was making my path clear for retreat? I had no inkling that what I was headed to, was much more harrowing than anything I was running from. I was running from a bad dream into a nightmare.

    I had left my cellphone behind at my brother-in-laws. I could not remember any of the phone numbers of anyone. Who was I going to call? I called the only person back home who I knew would help me, Renee. I reached her through the shelter hot-line and let her know when my plane would arrive and she picked me up at the airport.

She was bewildered. I couldn't seem to make her understand what had happened. Why should she understand, I did not understand it myself? I felt as if some uncontrollable force was directing my words and actions. I told her that I did not have a key to get into the house nor did I have a phone. She said that she would get a 911 cell phone for me like the ones which the center provided to crisis victims.

Renee had contacted my youngest daughter and she was waiting for me with a key when we arrived at my home. She handed me the key and with a look on her face which reflected years of our difficult relationship and anger mixed with confusion over my recent bizarre behavior, she said, "You cannot see your granddaughters again!" With that final, crushing statement, she turned and left.

In bewilderment, I opened the door, entered the house, shut the door tight, locked it and leaning against it in sheer exhaustion, let out a sigh of relief. I felt safe. I had no idea what was going to happen to me. I only knew I was home--back in the house, forgetting for a moment that this had been the very place where I had been besieged by mysterious illnesses.

Whatever was working in that house was not done with me yet. The snake was still lying in wait. I plummeted into a delusional hell. I did not feel safe. I felt as if something or someone was threatening me. I imagined that my husband wanted to kill me. I imagined that my daughter wanted to kill me. I imagined that they were in some bizarre plan together. I was losing it. I accused them of these horrible things.

    I don't remember all of the details of what I did during those few days in that house. I have been told that I called 911 too many times to count. The sordid things I dealt with at the Crisis Center became reality in my mind. I knew about crimes against women. I had all of this knowledge of all of the horrible crimes that could be perpetrated against humanity. I had seen with my own eyes the gory aftermath. I had heard the testimony of the victims. Satan used all of this knowledge and all of my own experiences to weave a macabre tapestry which began to hold sway in my mind.

    I believed Kent when he said that he was going to divorce me. I went to a lawyer. He informed me that my husband had indeed filed for divorce. This destroyed me inside. I left his office, went home, and began to sort through our belongings. I washed and ironed all of his clothes and began to lay them out with his other things. I sorted through hundreds of pictures of our life together. I was all alone. I knew that I would not be able to afford cable and internet services, so I began disassembling the computer and internet connections. I did not realize that when I pulled up the cable in the bedrooms I also had disconnected the phone service. I had no phone, no working cell phone, and no television. I continued to read my Bible and listen to Christian music on the radio but I was isolated. I had not held a driver's license for 6 years. I relied on the city bus service to travel around town. Years before

I had been appointed to the committee responsible for bringing public transportation to our city. Now, I was totally dependent on its services to function.

The buses only ran Monday through Saturday. In order to attend church, I had to use a taxi. Extremely early one Sunday, I walked the two blocks to the nearest gas station/convenience store to use the payphone to summon a taxi. I remember that the surreal feeling had intensified. I felt caught up in some sort of mental tornado. My senses already at a peak, seemed to increase their awareness of every sound, shape, and color. I remember feeling so much joy as I greeted the early risers who sporadically entered through the jingling door of the store. Most of the customers appeared to be dropping in for a coffee on their way to their various churches. I remember it as a rather pleasant experience although I sensed a feeling of impending…something. I remember engaging in a rather pleasant conversation with the taxi driver on our journey across town.

When we arrived at the entrance to the large church parking lot, the driver asked me if I wanted him to wait with me until someone arrived at the church. The building was dark inside. The lights from the enormous cross affixed to the front of the building together with the illuminated external baptismal fountain were to me comforting and welcoming. I assured the driver that I would be ok. He left and I was alone to walk about the grounds of the church. Eventually, one by one the members of the church and staff began to arrive. I was welcomed inside. It was a rather chilly morning I remember, unusual for August in West Texas.

The morning service is planned for the senior members of the church. The old-time country hymns being practiced by the boots-and-jeans-clad guitarist and fiddle player were comforting to my ears and my soul. I acknowledged a few familiar faces and was introduced to a few new ones. One of the familiar faces belonged to a woman who had been one of the founding volunteers who had donated her time and resources to renovate the shelter. I was drawn to her. I sat next to her and her husband for a time. I began to sense a dread the likes of which I had never experienced. I was overwhelmed with the sense that my youngest daughter was in danger. I began to cry. My agitation increased with each hymn. They no longer seemed to comfort me. I became obsessed with the idea that my daughter was in danger. My friend became alarmed at my behavior. I was swiftly veering out of control.

     In an effort to calm me, I was taken to the church office. The associate pastor, an extremely kind young man, began to ask me some questions about mundane things. He diverted my attention so that I did not at first realize that the security detail of the church, many of whom were police officers I had helped to train while at the center, had started to gather around me. I can only imagine what those police officers thought seeing me, the person who had been a part of their training and had worked alongside them responding to crisis calls now in such a confused state.

     The next thing I knew; I was being ushered down the corridors of the back of the church by a paramedic whom I also recognized. As I emerged from the darkness of the hallway into the bright sunlight, I saw the familiar red ambulance accompanied by the shiny red firetruck. How was this possible? I had not heard the usual sirens I had heard so many times before. It was eerily silent. The sympathetic smiles of the uniformed EMS workers and their downcast eyes seemed a strange form of reverence to me. I remember feeling that, finally, I was safe. I remember thinking that someone in the sky, up above the clouds was watching all of this transpire, some form of spiritual GPS.

    I remained in the emergency room alone and cold for what seemed like an eternity. I was hungry. It was now evening. I had only spoken to a few nurses throughout the day, no doctor. That seemed rather odd. I did receive a visit from an MHMR caseworker whom I had worked with on one of the Crisis Center cases. I thought, how nice of him to stop by, unaware that he was there to evaluate me. It was much later that I was told that I was being transported to the same hospital where I had been a patient when I had become emotionally distraught from the effects of the coma and drug withdrawal. I felt safe. I knew that place. It was a good place. As I emerged from the emergency entrance, I chuckled. The name on the transport bus read "Carol's Ambulance Service." I felt it was God's little sign.

    I remember talking with a very sweet intake worker at the facility. She assured me that everything was going to be all right. She did tell me a rather strange detail. She said that my daughter or someone who said that she was my daughter had visited the hospital just that week asking if I was a patient there. How bizarre.

I remember being escorted into the familiar lounge area of the adult ward. Now wearing a hospital gown, I was cold and tired. I slumped onto the couch and drifted off. I was awakened surrounded by several attendants whom I did not recognize. One of them held a huge syringe attached to what to me looked like a six-foot-long needle. They held me down which seemed peculiar because I was not resisting. As I drifted off, I remember thinking, is that what Ma meant when she called a shot a "hypo"? I remember smiling as I fell into unconsciousness.

I don't remember anything much about my stay. I don't even know for sure how long I was there. I only remember the day I left. I was asked to get dressed in one of the outfits which had been provided for me. A random pair of pants and slacks which I assumed had been donated to the hospital because they obviously were not new. I had no purse, no shoes, and no bra. They placed plastic restraints upon my wrists. My feet were shod with disposable foam slippers. I remember shuffling through the hallway past the nurses' station. I recall seeing the tear-stained face of the female doctor I had seen during my previous visit. I was enveloped in a haze. I distinctly remember her face as she silently mouthed the words, "I'm sorry." I thought that rather odd, yet I somehow understood.

I was placed in the back of some sort of official state vehicle. The honeycombed metal screen dividing the back seat from the front reminded me of all of the squad cars I had outfitted with emergency victim aid boxes. My mind fixated on the plush teddy bears and sweat suits placed inside the boxes to comfort the victims of horrific incidents. I wished that I had one of those teddy bears to hug, and the warm fuzzy sweat suit would have been welcomed, too.

The vehicle pulled away, and I was on my way to a place I had dreaded, feared ending up in my whole life-- a state hospital-- just like my mother. She had experienced a lifetime in and out of mental institutions. My mantra had always been, "I'm not going to be like my mother, I'm not going to be like my mother." Life with her was the stuff "lifetime" movies are made of.

Merriam Webster has two definitions for snake pit: a hospital for the mentally ill and a place or state of chaotic disorder and distress. Both of these definitions only begin to describe what became three weeks of fighting for my sanity. Satan had failed to steal, kill, and destroy my body. In fact, he had only given me a powerful testimony to God's healing powers. My detractors had already opened the doorway to the possibility that I was unbalanced, so the serpent must have decided that the best way to discredit my testimony was to convince people that I was crazy. Many years before I had read Joyce Meyer's book *The Battlefield of the Mind*. Little did I know that I would one day face combat with Satan in the battle for my own mind.

I can recall vividly each moment of that day and precisely my observations:

There were bars on the windows. There was a 20-foot-tall fence topped by razor wire surrounding the hospital grounds. It looked like a prison. The women's dormitory consisted of one long hallway with a nurses' station centrally located between the two wings. There were security cameras in the hallways and in all common areas. Each hallway had an assistant who constantly circulated in and out of each room, clipboard in hand, recording each and every move of the residents inside the rooms. There were never more than a few minutes in between each rotation. I was constantly watched. There was a huge flat- screen TV attached high on the wall in the lounge area. This is where I was allowed to watch TV and sometimes color in coloring books.

I was an art major when I began my studies at Indiana State University. Now, here in this place, I was doing something which I had thought too childish to do even when I was a child. Well-meaning relatives would invariably give me paint-by-number kits and coloring books when they learned that I liked to draw. I would politely thank them and then use their well-intentioned gifts as canvases for my own creations. Coloring inside the lines was never my strong suit.

My room housed me and three other women of varying ages and races. It was divided into four sections by large wooden cabinets with a side-by-side hanging closet attached to a chest of drawers. To the side of this chest of drawers was a small cubicle about waist high which held a small television. For the first two weeks I watched programs in silence because for some reason the sound would not work. No one told me until my second week as a patient that there were earphones available at the nurse's station. This small TV was my lifeline, my only connection to an important part of my past life-- NASCAR races. It was like Christmas to me when I once again could hear the thunder of engines as they circled the track.

I was born on Sunday morning, May 25, 1952, in Indiana. My daddy Bob, delighted in telling me that I was born just in time to hear the bells of our family church ringing in the distance. Back then, the Indianapolis 500 was run on Monday, the actual Memorial Day. My Sunday birth, Dad had told me, meant that he had plenty of time to rest up for "the race" on Monday.

When my father passed away, a huge part of my heart was buried along with him. He had been the only constant in my life, or so I thought at the time. Now here in this *place,* I had a piece of him with me. I tried to shut out the fact that NASCAR had also become a special bond to the other most important man in my life, my husband, Kent. But I couldn't bring myself to think about him. After all, hadn't I told the doctors that I thought he was trying to kill me? Hadn't I summoned police officers to my home to tell them exactly how I thought he was going to accomplish this deed? Hadn't I also told them that my daughter was also trying to kill me?

The morphine overdose had taken its toll on my memory. The only way I can describe it is that it is similar to the Nixon tapes: random spots of memory here and there had disappeared. Unfortunately, not only had the memory of some recent events been erased, but the recollection of events going as far back as six or seven years had vanished. Some of the incidents, I was glad I didn't remember, had disappeared, but tragically some of the most memorable times in my life were also gone forever. I seemed to mix together reality and things that were so bizarre that it was no wonder I found myself in this place.

The first room I was assigned was at the far end of one of the wings. I had befriended two women during the short time I had been there and one of them shared this space with me. One of the other two women in our room seemed to me to have nothing at all wrong with her except that she slept most of the day. She was very polite and a devout Catholic. The fourth woman in our room scared me. She talked to herself constantly, day and night. She would do so in a rather quiet voice for most of the time, muttering some bizarre language that seemed to include math equations. All night long this continued. The other woman whom I had befriended requested permission to change rooms. They only allowed you to do this one time. When she left, I was left with the Sleeper and the Mathematician.

The second day I was there. I received a summons to appear in the hospital's county courtroom. I boarded a van with other patients and was taken to the waiting room of the courtroom on the hospital grounds.

As I waited in silence for what I was not sure. I stared down at the piece of paper I had been given which informed me to appear at this time and this date. I had been in many courtrooms before serving as an advocate for crime victims but never like this. Today I was the one who was to appear. I looked around the room at the faces of the other people who were waiting. This place was for the insane I had been told. Some of them seem "normal" to me yet some seemed to fit the description of "insane."

There was one man who looked to be in his fifties sitting with his head hung down and grinding his teeth so loudly that it sounded like someone scraping a metal stool across a concrete floor. Each time we asked him to cease, he stopped for a few seconds and then returned to producing the monotonous din.

I had become somewhat acquainted with two of the ladies sitting close to me in the short time I had been a patient there. They seemed to be more aware of what was going to take place inside the courtroom. Luckily they were called in one at a time before me. From what I was able to ascertain, this hearing could determine how long I was to be "detained" in this facility. The trick I was told was that if you told the court that you feel you are well enough to be released, they would officially intervene and recommend that you be held for up to three months.

I was confused. I knew that I definitely did not want to remain there, but I also knew how the legal and medical insurance systems worked. I had good insurance, actually excellent insurance. Patients like me were few and far between in a state facility. I had a feeling I could be here for the duration of my allowable coverage. Painfully, I was right.

I was suddenly aware that they were calling my name. As I entered the courtroom, I was astounded to see so many grim faces glaring at me. I was directed to a small table in the back of the room. A man in a suit briefly introduced himself to me as my legal representative and seated himself beside me. I had never seen or talked to him before that moment. The judge at the front of the room addressed me and thanked me for making an appearance. (*I didn't know that I had a choice in the matter.)* He then began to address the side panel of men and women, mostly men, seated directly to my right. I had no idea what was to follow.

He began with, "As you can see, we have a fifty-seven-year-old white female who seems to be rather well composed and put-together. (Yes, I was put-together if anything else I knew that when you appeared in a courtroom you needed to look *put-together*. I had been up until 12:00 last night sorting through the bins of donated clothing which the hospital kept locked in a separate room in the dormitory. I helped the two women I had befriended prepare as well. I knew how to prepare a victim for the courtroom. I had done it many times. This time it was me preparing myself and them. They had been admitted to the hospital with some of their own clothing and personal items.

I had been transferred to this hospital with only one donated outfit from the previous hospital. Me, who once, routinely flew in the Dillard's private jet, wearing designer suits. Me, who had been a representative for one of the most prestigious and expensive cosmetic lines in the world. Me, who had dined in Four Star restaurants and worked with the likes of Neiman Marcus and Saks Fifth Avenue. *(Me, who sat here now, wearing borrowed makeup and donated clothes.)*

The judge continued, "She was transferred to our facility from a drug and alcohol treatment hospital with symptoms of extreme paranoia. She believes that her husband and daughter are trying to kill her." One of the few women on the panel asked me if this statement was true. I answered yes. *(Did I really say that? Did I sincerely mean that? It felt as though I did. I was afraid. But, of what, who)*

The Dr. assigned to me then went on to say, "She says that she was the director of a crisis center. She suffers from visions of grandeur."

I thought to myself, but I was the director. I tried to get the attention of my legal representative, but he motioned for me to be quiet.

The woman then asked me if I felt safe in this hospital and desired to remain. I remembered what I had been told. "If you say you think you should be discharged they will take the decision out of your hands and officially intervene and force you to stay for up to three months." Again I answer, "Yes."

The woman smiled and said, "Thank you. If you had said that you wanted to leave, we would have required you to stay." She seemed genuine.

The judge then decreed that I was to remain in the hospital for two weeks, during which time, I would be evaluated. The hearing was over.

For one full week, I was unable to sleep for more than a few moments at a time. My entire body was sore from trying to rest on the rock- hard mattress. The effects of two recent surgeries were still causing me physical discomfort. At last, I was supplied with a foam egg-crate mattress pad, which afforded some relief.

Each morning, noon, and night, all of us who wished to (medications were not mandatory) would line up behind the line at the clinic door by the nurses' station to receive our meds. After you took the pills they asked you to open your mouth to check that you had swallowed them. I had been prescribed only lithium, calcium, and magnesium supplements because my system was still depleted of those minerals. I remembered that my mother had been prescribed lithium to treat her illness. I had seen women pretend to swallow their meds when actually they would palm the pills or hide them behind their tongue. I wondered what they would do with them. Unfortunately, I would find out later.

The Mathematician's tirades were becoming more and more frequent and had become filled with rage. One evening shortly after I lay down to rest, she leaped from her bed and lunged at me, screaming at the top of her lungs. I ran from the room in fear of my life. The next day I asked to be moved. The nurse in charge warned me that I was entitled to only this one relocation. I asked to be moved to a room where three women were in residence. I moved. I felt safe in the new room, but only briefly.

I had no money only the "allowance" that you could earn each day if you attended classes, took a shower, washed your hair, did your laundry, and took your "meds."

Each day I was given paper printed with a checklist of my daily duties. As I completed each task, I was required to have a nurse assistant or classroom teacher witness the event and mark it off on her sheet and mine. At the end of the day, if I had been a good little girl, I was given my allowance the equivalent of $2.00 in paper certificates which could be redeemed in the canteen, beauty parlor or thrift shop. Sometime during my second week there, I noticed that one of my log sheets was missing. It was easily replaced and did not give the incident a second thought.

When I had entered the hospital, I had been allowed to pick out two outfits, shampoo, hair conditioner, deodorant, and one pair of shoes from the thrift shop and get one haircut from the beauty parlor. (My hair was falling out by the handfuls as a result of the overdose, the sudden cessation of six years of medication, and the myriad other recent shocks to my system. The beautician had to cut it off severely short to make it look even the least presentable. I looked like a peeled grape.)

This $2.00 was my allotment. Anything above this, I had to pay for. I had no money, no ID, no checkbook, no nothing except my faith. My purse and its contents had disappeared in the emergency room that Sunday of my meltdown. Two dollars a week was like a million dollars to me. I remember when I was able to buy my first 7-Up and a tube of Chapstick at the canteen. I remembered times when I wore and sold lipstick that cost $25.00 a tube. One of my new roommates worked part-time at the hospital, in the kitchen. I learned that long-term residents could earn this privilege. I wondered if I would be there long enough to qualify for a job.

I rested peacefully in the new room for only two nights. Suddenly during the third night, I was awakened by one of my new roommates. She stood above me completely naked, asking me if I would help her into her bra. I had been cordial to this woman, and other than her thinking that she was Janet Jackson, she had been quite pleasant. I had even helped her curl her hair.  But now   I was so startled that I screamed at the top of my lungs,

"Go away! Leave me alone!"

She awakened in me something I had never been able to express--the ability to scream out loud at the top of my voice, from my very soul, "GO AWAY, LEAVE ME ALONE." Never in my life of almost sixty years had I been able to stand up for myself in such a demonstrative way. As a child, I had always been the good girl.  Even when my family life was too much to bear, I could not tell anyone to stop, leave me alone. I was not able to speak out even when I was molested as a small child. I suffered the evil in silence.  It was then that I had first learned to physically run away.

It seemed to me that I now was running away in a different manner.  It seemed as though being here, in this place, I had run away, and now I wished to run away from the nightmare that was this place.

I ran to the nurse's station.  When I explained what had happened, they did not object.  They agreed to move me yet another time; no other questions were asked.    Later I discovered that the woman who had awakened me was a lesbian and it was not her first incident of this nature.

It was not always such chaos. God placed more than one woman who sought the Lord in my path during my stay there.  There was a woman in her late seventies who only wanted to be called "Reverend." She seemed to float through the hallways wearing, most of the time, a long black wool coat and various well-worn hats, a result of all being thrown into the washing machine every week.  She was particularly fond of one which bore a bright yellow tattered flower attached to the brim.  She was allowed to have a room to herself for many reasons, mostly because she had proven to be combative with a host of candidates for a roommate.  She was incoherent most of the time and mumbled in a low tone as she shuffled down the hallways.  Her room was kept at a sweltering eighty degrees at her request.

    Every Sunday we were allowed to go to Chapel if we wished.  On every Sunday that I was there but one, Reverend got all dressed up in her Sunday best and clutching her Bible walked the hallways toward our designated point of departure only to return to her room when the van arrived.  On one particular Sunday as we began boarding the van, Reverend finally joined us.  Once we entered the chapel, she took a seat in a pew about halfway down the outside aisle.

    Each Sunday the Chaplain asked if there was anyone who would like to sing.  This Sunday, I volunteered.  My voice was weak, the spirit inside me struggling to praise the Lord; it had been silent far too long.  I thumbed through the hymnal and found it, "Beautiful Savior."  As I finished singing, I noticed that Reverend had risen from her seat and was approaching an ancient upright piano which I hadn't even noticed, positioned on the side of the chapel, beneath a window.  The piano used for our services was a baby grand on the stage at the front of the room.  No one seemed to be aware of what was happening, but the chaplain acted as if he was expecting what was to come.

    Silently, Reverend pulled the wooden bench out from under the piano and sat down.  She looked as if she had done this a million times before.  Then she began to manipulate the keys, and the resulting melody was reminiscent of a true Baptist revival. "Rock of Ages" was never played with more passion. That chapel rocked with pure Gospel music. When it was over, Reverend stood up, left the piano, and slipped quietly back into the pew and into blank silence. For a brief moment, she had touched my soul. She made me rejoice.

From that day forward, she let me into her world. She even allowed me to enter her room, something the nurses said was rare. On one occasion, she took me over to her dresser and began to search for something. She finally found it—the hat with the yellow flower.

She began to pinch and shape it, and when she was satisfied, placed it on my head. She then lifted her long black coat and held it out for me to try on. It was heavy thick scratchy wool and smelled of sweat. I didn't mind. She was offering me something that meant a lot to her. We connected. I walked the hall with her that day. I was honored.

Somewhere at some time, this woman had a place in her church. She was an integral part of it. Somehow she had become lost in the world in which she now lived. Her family, proud and caring, visited her often. She was loved.

Reverend was not the only lost soul I befriended there. Another friend was almost 6 feet tall and muscular. She was legally blind and therefore unable to read. She craved the Bible. She craved any piece of literature she could find which pertained to God's Word. She was a soul in search of forgiveness. She had been entangled in the world of pornography and sex. She herself had acted in pornographic movies. She had become a prostitute on the streets of Dallas where she contracted AIDS. She became homeless and, when her mind began to fade, was placed in this hospital.

AIDS had begun to deteriorate her eyesight and her brain. She had episodes of horrendous delusion. She would have horrible dreams that she was engaging in lesbian activity. It disgusted her. I was reminded of the children's song, "Be Careful Little Eyes What You See."

Once you see or do unclean things, they are forever imprinted on your mind. Random thoughts of what you have witnessed or participated in can pop up into your consciousness at any given time. They can impede your ability to feel in the way in which God intended your sexual self to live. Your thought innocence is taken away. Sexual sins alter your healthy sexual life. Satan the serpent uses those sins to invade this gift that God intended for us to use to his glory. I know these things because I had succumbed to the sexual lures of Satan.

My friend craved forgiveness. She craved the Bible. She held her well-worn Bible so close to her face that it caressed her cheek. Sometimes at night when I couldn't sleep, I would find her in the lounge. Spread about her were pamphlets from numerous evangelists. We would sit for hours, wherever we could find a place to plant ourselves, and talk about Jesus. She could not believe that God had forgiven her of her many sins. Each time she asked this question, I assured her that if she had sincerely asked God to forgive her, He had. She would stare at me as if she was trying to remember if she had indeed been sincere. She constantly asked me if I had any maps of the Holy Land. I told her that I would try to find her one. Sometimes she would stop me in the hallway. "Let's read," she would say. So right then and there, we would drop down, sit cross-legged on the floor, and read the Bible until she was satisfied. When I was allowed to use the computer in the library, I copied and enlarged various maps of the ancient Holy Land and gave them to her.

The last room I resided in was occupied by three women, one of whom was still wearing a white bandage covering her wrists, a telltale reminder of her attempted suicide. She had resorted to such a drastic measure in an effort to escape the horrors of severe domestic abuse, quite like the many cases I had witnessed while running the Crisis Center. There in that cold, stark room illuminated by the gray light of the cloudy day beyond the steel-mesh-covered windows, we laughed and cried together.

It struck me that I was not quite sure if the barriers placed on the windows were there to keep us inside these walls or if they served to shield us from whatever had been haunting us on the outside. Through her tears, she managed at last to smile faintly.

This was not my first encounter with the ugliness of domestic violence during my sojourn here. One of the women who became a resident the second week of my stay bore the marks of repeated physical abuse. She tried to hide the bruises by wearing long-sleeved sweaters and skirts that flowed to the ground. It was August in West Texas. The heat was sweltering. She wore thick cotton socks to cover her shins, which were marked from ankle to knee in bruises where she had been kicked repeatedly. She wore her hair long, the strands of unwashed tendrils hiding most of her face, a sort of mask. No makeup, no smile, no expression. She did not even respond to me the first couple of times I tried to speak to her. She stared at the floor in silence. I had seen this look many times when I worked with the women in Angel House.

I found a way to reach her. When I was allowed to go through the clothing donations, I would find small sizes I thought would fit her and would leave them neatly folded at the end of her bed. I was always delighted when I saw her wear them. Gradually I was able to get her to answer me when I said hello or simply asked how she was doing. Soon she began to open up to me about her situation. It was dismal but nothing I hadn't heard many times before. Eventually, she started to fix her hair and wear just the slightest touch of makeup. We would sometimes sit late at night and chat about nothing in particular. It was like watching a rosebud begin to unfold.

I received a notice that I had been granted another hearing. The same procedure that I had undergone on the previous occasion was repeated. The two women I had accompanied to the first hearing and I began our get-ready preparations. Once again we went through the donations to find something that would make us look as if we were ready to rejoin society. We rehearsed bits of information such as who the President of the United States was and anything I thought we might be asked which would indicate that we were aware of our surroundings or at least what year, month and day it was.

The day of the hearing we again boarded the van which took us to the chapel building where the courtroom was located. Again we waited. When it was my turn, I slowly arose from my seat and with each measured step I silently prayed, "Lord, please let me go home."

It was not to be so. The same doctor who had seemed so intent on keeping me there in the hospital, again stated that he felt I needed further observation. My mind cried out, observation for what? I was better, wasn't I? I had been a good little girl.

Inside I screamed at the top of my soul, "I want to go home!" Then I remembered I had two more weeks of insurance coverage. There was no way I was going to be released until my insurance was up. The flawed system of mental facilities that keeps a patient in residence only until their insurance coverage lapses and then declares them cured or healed was present and working. I returned to my room and cried.

Soon after that day, while I was standing at the medication door waiting for my meds, the pharmacy nurse made a sharp statement that he was not allowed to deliver my medication and that I was to report to the head nurse. I patiently waited outside her office until she opened the door and ushered me inside. In utter astonishment, I listened as she asked me a question that to this day was beyond my belief. "Are you selling drugs here in the hospital?"

I was appalled and dumbfounded. How could they think that I would or could do such a thing? Through tears of disbelief, I asked her why someone would accuse me of such a thing. She said, "Honey, you've got to remember where you are."

I had become very fond of this particular nurse. She reminded me of my best friend back home. She made me feel safe. She worked nights and would often be the one to try to get me to go to sleep on those long periods when my back and legs kept me up. Now she told me that I needed to talk to my caseworker about the drug accusations.

The next day I made the request for a meeting with my caseworker. I had only seen her briefly during a panel session. At that time one of the doctors had asked me various questions about why I felt that my life was in danger and if I knew why I was there. I had only been in the hospital a few days at that point and was still in a state of mental confusion. I remember that then I really did feel as if my life was being threatened. Maybe what I had been feeling was as if my life as I had known it was being threatened. I still don't really understand it all and don't know if I ever will.

During this meeting, I anxiously retold the events of the previous day. I made sure she knew that I would never, ever do such a thing as sell drugs. At that time the only medication I was receiving was calcium, lithium, magnesium and the occasional Tylenol for leg cramps. How could I acquire the drugs I was accused of selling? She immediately calmed me with the assurance that she and the doctors knew that I had not done what I was accused of. She said that they had found one on my daily duty sheets and on it was written the drugs I was accused of selling and the cost of each. She pulled the missing sheet from her folder and handed it to me. I couldn't believe what I saw. At the top of the sheet, in a jagged handwriting were the names of several drugs and how much each would cost.

My caseworker went on to explain that she knew that it was not my handwriting because she had samples of my writing from the suggestion, and Employee of the Month boxes in the lobby.

I had been very dutiful in placing my suggestions and nominations in those boxes since the second week I was there. I knew how much I had depended on these inventions when I had run the center. On one occasion a nurse had taken me aside and thanked me for my observation concerning one of the ward assistants. She assured me that there would be no repercussions from the situation I had revealed. I didn't understand what she meant by repercussions. Then it hit me. I had reported that the assistant was a lesbian and had been recruiting other staff members and patients to join her. I had also witnessed her being physically abusive to one of the other aides. I had not realized that what I had done was dangerous. I did now and I was scared.

God revealed to me that through my desire to expose a dangerous injustice and in another instance tell of someone's kindness to me, that He had opened an avenue to rescue me from the snare. It was as though through my written words of testimony; I had been saved from my circumstance. The words of John 8:32 NIV are so true: "Then you will know the truth, and the truth will set you free."

I had finally allowed the doctors to contact Kent, and one week before I was released, he delivered a suitcase to the hospital. At last, I had some of my own clothes. It was like a million Christmases all rolled into one. Tucked away in a corner of the suitcase was my Bible-- at least it looked like my Bible on the outside. Inside it was a different story. The pages were marred with all sorts of handwriting which I recognized as my own. But most of the words seemed unfamiliar. I barely remembered writing some of the phrases in the margins of the text. From what I could gather, I had been writing the names of people who had done harm to me in my life. Sometimes I had written why I felt that I had deserved such treatment.

Why would I treat God's Holy word with such irreverence? All my life I had treated the Bible as if it was made of pure gold. I had been given His Word in various forms all my life. I still have the Bible I was given when I was confirmed. I had cherished a mother of pearl edition from the Holy Land given to me by a wonderful Christian woman. What horrendous evil spirit could have possessed me to make me do such things? While I continued to inspect my Bible, I began to smile. I had to do something. Towards the back, just past Revelation, I found it. The map of the Holy Land. I quickly took it to the nurses' station and asked them to make an enlarged copy. When I presented it to my friend, I knew why it had been returned to me.

I quickly changed from the donated clothing to my own familiar garments. I almost felt like my old self...whatever that was. I found some belts which had obviously eluded the inspection of the nurses.

Thankfully the next few days held some much awaited good news. The doctor who had for some reason been adamant about my continued residency there was going on vacation. The doctor who now presided over my care was soon to become my rescuer. He listened to the therapist who had been sympathetic to my pleas that I did not belong there. She had pled my case to the new doctor, and he listened. I was summoned to a meeting of the two. During this session, I was asked some very key questions.

One, did I feel that I was in danger from my husband or my daughter? My answer was a truthful no. I couldn't for the life of me remember why I would have ever thought that possible. How could I have been the one who had acted in such a manner?

The therapist asked me what I had done professionally before I became sick. I again stated that I had been the executive director of The Crisis Center and Angel House in Odessa. She smiled and assured the doctor that she had spoken to my husband and this was indeed the case. She said that she also served as a champion of people in trouble. We shared a knowing smile. The doctor shut my file, shook his head, and firmly stated the sweetest words I believe I had ever heard, "We've got to get you out of here. You don't belong here."

He instructed the therapist to get started with the plans for my release. It would still take a few days. Freedom was within reach, but just where was I going to go? I couldn't call my husband. I couldn't call my daughter in Odessa. I did not have my daughter in Houston's number. I did not have money for a long distance call. I was only allowed one phone call a week. Calls to my sweet cousin Judy in Indiana had been my only lifeline, but she and her husband Ray were raising her granddaughter Ashley, who has special needs. They were not equipped to handle me in the fragile state I was in, although I knew that they would have tried. My oldest daughter living in Houston had called me and even sent me socks when I told her how cold I was in the hospital. She had even sent money to be deposited in my account, but I never knew it. I did not wish to impose myself upon her and her husband. The phone calls from these few people were all I had to hold on to. Where was I going to go? I had no money. No home. No friends (or so I thought).

For some reason, the doctor had decided that I needed a new medication. I questioned this order but remembered that if you refused to obey the orders, your stay would be lengthened. The new medication was very strong. It seemed to make me feel worse instead of better. I felt as if I was taking a giant step backward. Each day my mental fuzziness seemed to increase.

Why would they give me something which made me feel worse? Up until this time, I had only been given lithium and calcium and magnesium. Why now, so far into my stay there and with my release only days away, would they do this to me? This question would only be answered later, upon my release, when I discovered that it was standard operating procedure to administer this medication to all patients prior to release to reduce the risks of disruptive behavior upon return to the population.

Satan the snake had been good at convincing me that I was alone. That mindset had successfully turned me into a solitary victim that served as his perfect prey.

# CHAPTER 10

## THE RAISED SERPENT

Numbers 21: 8-9 NKJ

> Then the Lord said to Moses, "Make a fiery *serpent*, and set it on a pole; and it shall be that everyone who is bitten, when he looks at it, shall live." [9] So Moses made a bronze serpent, and put it on a pole; and so it was, if a serpent had bitten anyone, when he looked at the bronze serpent, he lived.

FRIDAY, THE DAY of my release came, and again. following standard operating procedure, I was given a bus ticket, taken to the bus station, and herded onto a packed bus headed west. I was met at the station in Odessa by two caseworkers from the local mental health office, two people I had worked cases with in the past. They had been given instructions to take me to one of the cut-rate hotels in Odessa and to pay for one night's stay. I had worked cases at those hotels. They were full of drug dealers and other assorted criminals, not a place where I would feel safe, but I had no money, no identification, just a few articles of clothing crammed inside one solitary suitcase.

I convinced the pair to take me to my bank. I will never forget the woman who helped me that day. Joanna had been my banker for years. By allowing me to access my personal account, she rescued me. I quickly withdrew funds and was taken by the caseworkers to a hotel adjacent to the bank. I secured a room and carried the suitcase holding all of my belongings up to the room which would be my home for the next two days. I literally jumped into the huge fluffy, king- sized bed, a stark difference from what had been my resting place for the past three weeks.

But where would I go from here? I still felt as if I had no one I could contact. I was out of that nightmare of a hospital. but what would I face tomorrow?

It was now September, and I had only a pair of sandals to wear. I had no means of transportation, so I knew that I would be walking wherever I needed to go. The hotel was located close to the mall in Odessa, so I walked the short two blocks and purchased a new pair of tennis shoes. I knew that I had to watch my money because there was very little remaining in my bank account.

The next day, Saturday, I rested. I must have slept until noon. On Sunday I called a cab and proceeded to the very church where I had suffered my breakdown. I contacted one of the pastors there, told him of my circumstance. and asked for help in finding a place to live. He had his wife take me back to the hotel. I was on my own.

Without my cell phone, I still had no way to access the numbers of anyone I knew. Then it hit me-- I remembered one of my friends from the past, Marsha, the sister of the man I had intended to marry when I moved back to Odessa. We had remained friends for over twenty years. I searched the phonebook for her number; to my relief she was still listed. When she answered the phone her familiar voice brought tears to my eyes. When I explained to her my situation, she immediately came to the hotel and took me back with her to her home. For the first time in months, I felt relief. She opened her home to me and it became my safe-haven.

There was a lot to be done, many appointments to be kept. With no driver's license, much less a vehicle, it was necessary for me to use taxis and busses. I believe that it was also God's way of allowing me to experience what it was like to be homeless. I had been a part of the Homeless Coalition and as such had been involved in needs assessment round-ups where we targeted places where homeless people congregated. I was finding out first-hand what their needs were, but I was blessed-- I had a place to sleep, due to the kindness of a friend.

One Sunday afternoon as I was sitting at the dining room table, enjoying a dinner with Marsha's family, her phone rang. It was my oldest daughter, calling me from Houston. I grabbed the phone from Marsha and ran to the bedroom. When I heard her voice on the other end of the call, I began to sob. Her words, "I love you Mom," were like a lifeline to me. When I finished our conversation, I ran back into the dining room and shouted, "She loves me, my daughter loves me!" I was not alone.

My emotional state during that time had resembled the ups and downs of a roller coaster. I was still finding it difficult to sleep. One evening after I had taken the medication I had been prescribed when I was dismissed from the hospital, my heart began to race, beating so loudly that I felt as if it was going to burst from my chest. I fell to the bathroom floor in a sweaty clump. That was the last time I took that medication.

Slowly I began to resemble the person I had been six years before. I was getting stronger. I began attending a small mission church and with Marsha's son's family, even visited the church where I had suffered my breakdown. I had stayed at Marsha's much longer than either of us had planned. Being unemployed with only disability income had been an obstacle in obtaining an apartment, but finally, I was able to secure a small two-room space located on one of the bus routes.

My divorce was still in process, and the date of the final hearing was fast approaching. I had no contact with Kent since I had escaped from Dallas that day except for a preliminary divorce hearing. Our lawyers were busy working out the numerous details of the final settlement.

I was alone in that tiny apartment, alone with God. He and I did a lot of talking. I did a lot of praying. Then for the third time in my life, I found myself thrown down on the floor.

The first time was only two years into Kent's and my marriage, the first time we had separated and were headed for a divorce. That time the episode began late one night just a few months before the mysterious illnesses began. I was alone in my office at the Center, working on a grant. Suddenly I became terrified with a feeling that I could not go home. My step-daughter, who I now felt was my own, had just moved in with us and it had been one of the happiest periods of our marriage thus far so I was bewildered as to why I felt terror at the thought of going home. The fear escalated, my heart raced, I could feel it beating in my head.

I grabbed the phone and called my G.P.'s answering service. When she called me back, I told her what I had been experiencing. She replied, "Well Carol, you know what I have to ask you. I know you ask the same questions of your crisis clients. Do you feel like hurting yourself?" "Do you feel like hurting anybody else?" To each of these questions I replied a truthful, NO." She then told me that there was nothing that she could do for me but if I felt the same tomorrow to call her.

I hung up the phone and slumped down in my chair. The feeling of fear increased to the point where I called Kent and told him that I was not coming home, I would be at my daughters.

*How I wish that I had known then what I know now, I didn't need to call a doctor, I needed to pray.*

I did not call my doctor next day, instead, I stayed at my daughter's for several weeks during which time, I filed for divorce. It is hard for me to talk about this time, it seems as if it was happened to someone else. It felt like someone had taken control of my will and was driving me down paths not of my choosing. I had rented a house with an option to buy and it was there, on the floor, beside the new bed I had purchased, a bed that would soon be moved back into the home I shared with Kent when we reconciled, the same bed where I would be stricken with the beginning of my illness. The first time I found myself lying face down, arms spread wide, completely surrendered. I felt a force pushing me to the floor. The words I heard were,

"I do not want this marriage to end. This is MY marriage!".

It took me several days to work up the courage to call Kent. When I did, I asked him to meet with me. He asked a mutual good friend, Gilda, to serve as a go-between because we both trusted her ability to give us her honest opinion and advice about our situation. After listening to our conversation and my heartfelt apology to Kent for causing him such heartache, she prayed with us and told Kent that she believed me. What I had not known, was that before our meeting that day, Kent had told her that he did not know if he could forgive me for running out on him. When his first wife had left him, it nearly destroyed him. She asked him, "What does it say in Matthew 18:22 about forgiveness? I believe it says to forgive seventy times seven, Little Brother!" We reconciled a few days after that meeting, only a few days before the final hearing.

At that time, the fact that I became ill only a few months after moving back into our home had been the impetus for one of my family members with a vivid imagination and a sincere concern for my well-being to call my doctor and alert her to their bizarre suspicion that possibly Kent was poisoning me. Following procedure, she had called me and asked me to come to her office to have my blood drawn so that this accusation could be put to rest. *Could this have been when the seed was planted in my thoughts that Kent was trying to kill me?*

It was shortly after that reconciliation that a force, not from God, threw me to the floor when the attack upon my physical body launched me into the six years of illness.

Now, alone in my tiny apartment, this time, once again I felt a force pull me from my bed, throwing me to the floor. Again, face down, I heard the same words, "I do not want this marriage to end. This is my marriage!" But this time the words were followed with, "Call him."

How could I call him? Surely he would hang up on me. Regardless, I obeyed. My fingers were shaking as I dialed his cell number, the only number I had memorized. He answered, and his voice to me sounded like an angel's voice. He didn't hang up. I couldn't believe it! He didn't hang up! That phone call led to countless others until shortly before Christmas, we finally agreed to meet.

I felt like a teenager about to go on her first date. He came to my apartment, and we sat for hours talking. We both were dumbfounded as to how we had reached this point. Amid all of the discussion, it was clear-we both still loved each other. We knew that we would be facing many obstacles if we were to get back together. Except for my cousin, my oldest daughter, and Kent's father, sister and brother-in-law, just about everyone had advised Kent to get rid of me. My own brothers urged him to divorce me, saying that I was crazy like our mother and that I would never change. We knew that if we were to reconcile, we would be virtually on our own.

We canceled our divorce proceedings one week before the final hearing. I moved back to our home, and we began to heal our marriage. It took a while to feel comfortable back in the house where I had suffered so much sickness, but it did not take long for us to realize that our marriage had been ordained by God for a special purpose.

In time most of our family began to re-establish contact with us. While we were busy rebuilding our marriage, I began to rebuild my life. The first thing on the agenda was to obtain my driver's license. I had not been behind the wheel of a car for six years. I believe that I was more nervous this time around than I had been when I was sixteen. With license in hand, I began to seek a part-time job. I secured a substitute teaching position and gradually got back into the swing of a somewhat normal life. We began attending church regularly and enjoyed making new Christian friends.

When we occasionally ran into some of our old acquaintances who had not seen me since I had been healed, the astonished looks on their faces would sometimes be followed with a, "Oh my God, I thought you were dead!" They were right--the old me was dead. This new creation, this resurrected me, was filled not only with the Holy Spirit but also with a new purpose. That purpose was to proclaim the miracle healing of God in my life. One woman whom I had not known before approached me one day and said that she had been told to find me and to see the miracle. God had a plan.

September of 2012, I was once again up on the mountain in New Mexico at camp for a women's retreat. That year I was a part of the praise team and was scheduled to be the guest speaker two years later. Sleeping in the dorm as I had done so many times before, usually serving as dorm mom *(how prophetic)*, I was awakened for one of my usual 3 AM meetings with my Daddy, God. This time there were no immediate words from Him, so I grabbed my laptop and began working on the manuscript for this book. As I was writing, the message finally came,

"Sweetheart, now I want you to take all of the things I have allowed you to learn here on earth, all of the dark alleyways you have traveled, all of the things you have learned in the business world, and use them for My Business, bringing souls to Me."

Then, I heard the words, My Father's Business. Later that morning during chapel, as the camp director, Rusty began delivering his sermon, he quoted the scripture which is centered on the time when Jesus was a young boy and his mother and father could not find him. When they finally went to the temple searching for him, they found him teaching the teachers, this is what he replied:

Luke 2:49 KJV "And he said unto them, How is it that ye sought me? wist ye not that I must be about my Father's business?"

That was my confirmation. That scripture explained the good that God could bring out of my crazy zig- zag, snake- path life. My dream job was ahead, working for the greatest boss in the world, my Daddy, my Father God.

In 2012, we began looking for a new home. We discovered one being built adjacent to our church. The builder, had not intended to sell it. Odessa was in the middle of one of its notorious economic booms, and he was building this house as a corporate rental property. One day, after praise team practice, I asked our worship leader and a few close friends from the Praise Team to join me as I prayed over the wooden beams which had recently been erected on the foundation of the house. I grabbed a wooden beam in each of my hands and prayed that if God allowed us to purchase this home, it would serve as an open- door ministry. Anyone who needed a place to stay would find it here.

God listened. With a little persuasion by our realtor, who was a Christian, the builder agreed to sell to us. He, along with over fifty of our close friends. wrote their blessing and favorite scriptures on the foundation.

The day we moved in, the cleaning crew was just finishing up with the final touches. I began talking with the woman who, along with her family, was employed by our builder to prep all of his properties. As I watched her daughter mop the floor, I told the woman what was written on the concrete underneath the tile she was cleaning. She smiled and said to her daughter, "I told you so." She went on to tell me that she had always felt a kind of peace when she entered this house, so much so that if she was having a bad day while working in the surrounding houses in the complex, she would walk over to our house and simply touch the outside wall and feel at peace.

We knew that our home had been blessed by God. We felt it too. We also began to talk for the first time about how we had felt the presence of something evil in our old house. Kent said that on occasion he would feel as if someone was standing behind his chair as he sat in the living room and, thinking it was me, would turn to find no one there. We believed the evil presence was real. We also realized that it had almost succeeded in destroying our marriage and my life.

Our new home soon became a hub of activity. We hosted a small group which at times grew to be not so small. There was a well-worn path between our home and the church building used not only by our small group but also the youth group, who knew that they could always hang out and find something good to eat there. Kent and I had continued to support the youth of the church with Kent making his twice-yearly pilgrimages to the Guadalupe mountains for youth camp. Years before, he had been given the nickname "Phat Daddy," which did not refer to his size but was at that time a term of endearment. I had become "Mama Sue", a title bestowed upon me by our daughter's dance team friends. Together we set about following the leading of God. We knew He had a purpose for keeping our marriage together, and with each day we discovered new reasons why.

Our oldest granddaughter, came to live with us for a brief time. A few years earlier when we were moving into our new home, both granddaughters had engaged in a humorous battle over which room in the house was theirs. Now, under unexpected circumstances the room they had fought over belonged to the oldest.

After a very challenging four months, she ran away; a behavior I was all too familiar with. I cried for three days, and then sitting alone on our sofa, I heard God's voice speak to me.

"But if you had the desire of your heart, you wouldn't be available for what I need you to do."

I had no idea what He needed for me to do. I wouldn't know for several more months. I knew what He meant by the desire of my heart—my granddaughter. I desperately desired to hold her again, to keep her safe. In Psalms 37:4, it says "Delight thyself also in the LORD; and he shall give thee the desires of thine heart. I had to trust God that He had my granddaughter, the desire of my heart, in His hands. I had to trust that He had a reason for this particular circumstance.

One Sunday morning there was a guest speaker at church, Brent, who was a young missionary who had begun a ministry called Rescue Innocence a program to end human trafficking. I felt this to be ironic for he seemed to me to be such an innocent himself. I remember thinking that day that he reminded me of my younger brother, the one whom I had thought would one day accompany me to Africa. I was immediately compelled by the Holy Spirit to go to him and pray protection over him. From experience, I knew that the details of what he would be facing, the evil that was present in the sex trade, could attempt to latch on to him and drag him down into the pit I had encountered. I did pray for him that day, and it was the beginning of a deep friendship. Through the course of our friendship, I learned that he was also was a part of an organization called Uganda Now Outreach. I thought back to the vision God had given me in the coma.

One day when he was visiting our home, he began to talk to me about Africa and how he needed to make another trip very soon. Our church had raised money to dig wells and build a much-needed clinic there in the villages of Makindu and Busagazi. He stopped what he was saying and looked at me. His next words were, "I think it's time for you to go to Uganda with me."

There it was. The vision became reality; God had planned this moment years ago, possibly even before I was born. Plans were made, I received all the necessary inoculations and all was made ready.

About two months before our scheduled departure, while on a phone call to Brent in Missouri, where he was headquartered, I felt compelled to ask him what we would do for music while in Uganda. He said that they had only a set of drums in each location though one set was in bad condition. He played the guitar, and we decided that we needed to take a one with us as a gift to be used for worship. I contacted one of our local music stores, and happily, they supplied not one but two guitars, one of which had been donated by one of their customers. That particular guitar was electric, not much use in the bush country of Uganda where there was no electricity.

God knew all along that He would bring to us, before we left for Uganda, another missionary who owned a radio station which broadcast the message of Jesus into the Congo. The day he visited our church was the exact day that Brent and I were there showing the church what a great blessing God had provided for our trip. When we saw the look on the visiting missionary's face as he gazed at the beautiful black and white instrument, we knew what God had intended all along. We had no natural way of knowing that this missionary had been praying for just such a guitar. The guitar was meant for his ministry, not ours and with great joy it was given and received.

One day Brent called me and told me that someone had donated some makeup. He asked me if I thought that we could use this donation in Uganda. Almost laughing, I told Brent that I had not told him of one of my former lives; my life in the cosmetic industry. Oh yes, we definitely would be able to use this generous gift.

I had become close to one of the leaders of our church, Frankie, a woman whom I felt had become my spiritual mom. Although she was only a few years older than I, her wisdom in matters of the Holy Spirit made her seem to me to be like what the Bible refers to as a "Wise Man", a description which gave me mental image of an aged man with a long flowing beard. She was certainly not an aged man but a stylish woman who simply glowed with the joy of the Lord. I wanted what she had, that joy, that presence. Frankie began to open my eyes to who the Holy Spirit is. I had no idea who He is. My early church- school education only left me with the knowledge that He is part of the Triune God and that he was born on Pentecost, a day we honored in Sunday school by wearing tiny paper flames on top of our heads. He seemed to me to be clouded in mystery along with the book of Revelation which we were told was too difficult for us to understand at our young age.

It was Frankie who had led me to the knowledge of the gifts of the Spirit. She was the one who prayed with me the day I received the gift of tongues, July 5, 2013, just four days before I was to leave for Uganda. Frankie, her husband Calvin, my dear friend Miss.

Melba and I had been gathering at our church each day at noon and praying for the nation during Anne Graham Lotts, Seven Days of Prayer for Our Nation. This particular Friday was different. I had been praying for several months that God would give to me the gift of tongues. Brent and Frankie had both forewarned me that I would be facing all sorts of evil spirits in Africa and that I must prepare to fight them. I had been warned that Voodoo and devil worship are thriving there.

That Friday, July 5, 2013, while standing at the front of a church which does not embrace the gifts of tongues, those three believers prayed over me that the Holy Spirit would descend upon me. The next thing I knew; I was on the floor. It felt as if a huge ball of something was welling up in my stomach. This mass seemed to travel through my throat and with a force, began spewing out of my mouth in a barrage of syllables that sounded like a language which was both strange and familiar at the same time.

I was spent, lying limp on the floor sweating, crying and laughing all at the same time. I was overcome with a burning desire to climb up the steps to the stage above me and begin beating on the conga drum used by the Praise Team., but I was too weak and exhausted to even raise my head. I remember thinking as the three helped me to my feet, "OK. How does this work? Will this happen this way every time? Will I be able to control this?" But I did not have time to think about all of these details. I had only four more days to prepare for the trip.

Now I knew who had been speaking to me all these years. The voice I heard on the plane, at Neiman

Marcus, and in the car driving back to New Orleans, had been the Holy Spirit whispering to my soul. Now I knew who was living inside of me. Now I knew who was churning up the desire in me to spread the knowledge of Jesus to the world.

It was time to go. I boarded a plane, guitar strapped to my back, suitcases filled with medical supplies donated by my son-in-law's father, and headed off to Africa to join Brent and Alan, a young man from his church.

The six hundred joyful children waiting for us there were a blessing beyond my wildest imagination. There in Africa, in the bush country of Uganda, God fulfilled His vision to me. As I stood and watched Brent, this young man from my vision, teach the young men of the school how to play the guitar, I thought, how great is our God! He is faithful in His promises.

While I was in Uganda, something kept nagging at me. Surely, I thought, I did not travel around the world simply to be blessed to meet these beautiful children and Christine and Deo, the missionary couple who run the schools. I didn't want to believe that I was sent there merely to roll a few stripes of paint on the walls of the new clinic, a task we knew had already been planned. Anyone could have done that. Why was I, there? Then it happened.

Immediately upon arrival in Entebbe, we began to organize our plans for next 10 days. Christine asked me if we planned on providing a feast for the children explaining that it was only when missionaries came that most of the children had the opportunity to eat meat.

Kent and I had provided all of the necessary funds to cover my expenses for the mission from our own finances. We had also managed to tuck away a small amount of money in a separate account, for no specific reason. Kent had said, "You'll know what to do with it when the time comes." The time had come.

I asked Christine how much a feast would cost for 600 children and their teachers. She began to recite all of the necessary ingredients needed to complete the menu, "First we will need to kill a cow, then buy the beans and rice, and if you think we will be able to afford it, the children would love to have some juice."

I asked her to figure out the cost of all of those items and I would see if we had enough money to cover it. She pulled out her notebook and began to make her calculations. When she showed me the final figure that was required, my heart ascended about a foot up my chest and lodged somewhere that prevented me from speaking for a moment. The amount of money Kent and I had set aside for, "you'll know it when the time comes," was $356.00. The amount needed to feed 600 was $353.00. I began to think about loaves and fishes.

Upon my return to Texas, I couldn't wait to tell Kent my story of our, "Feeding the Six-Hundred." He laughed and, as usual joked, "You know, if we're gonna be in the cattle business, you can't kill the first cow we buy!"

The second confirmation of why God had called me to Uganda occurred a few days later just as I had finished delivering my testimony to the women and some of their husbands. I was standing outside one of the school buildings in the shade of a huge tree when one of the women approached me. She lived in one of the tiny mud huts which were standing nearby. She told Christine that she needed to speak with me. She spoke only Ugandan, so Christine interpreted. She said that she didn't think that God could forgive her for her great sin. She went on to explain the details of what she felt was her great sin, and the words pierced my heart. She had been carrying the same burden of what I felt had been one of my greatest sins. I could see that this burden had weighed her down just as it had me for a time. Her face revealed so much to me. Her downcast eyes spoke volumes. She felt that a decision she had made was in the best interest of her child, just as I had done many years ago. Now she felt the burden of that decision and that God could not forgive her.

I asked her if she had asked God to forgive her, and she replied that she had. I then told her that God had indeed forgiven her, that it was only she who was holding on to the sin. I told her to let it go. Then I began to pray for her, in English. As I began with the second phrase, I began praying in tongues. This was only the second time this had happened to me. The first was only a few days before I got on the plane to come to Africa. I remember wondering at the time how this thing worked, how or would it happen again, but I had been so caught up in preparations for my trip that I had not given it much thought.

Then it happened, as I was praying in The Spirit, Christine ceased to interpret, but the woman seemed to understand what the Spirit was saying to her. As tears began to fall gently down her cheeks, she smiled, her tears of joy sparkling in the African sun. As we hugged each other, both of us crying now, I told her that each night when she looked up at the moon, just know that I am a world away looking at the same moon, that we would forever be connected like a triangle with God at the top, in heaven.

    I knew then that my trials and the testimony of God's deliverance from them, had made a difference to this African child of God.  My mission there was to proclaim His goodness, His miraculous healing in my life.  Standing outside of the mud huts in sweltering heat, I lifted up the healing serpent.

    God does not waste one single element of your testimony.  Later that day, in the bush country of Africa, Christine and I conducted our version of "Beauty Makeovers."  I placed my suitcase containing the cosmetic samples on the crumbling porch of the school building.  Broad smiles and squeals of glee erupted as I opened the case revealing its contents.  Christine organized the women into two lines.  She set up a table at the head of one line and I did the same at the other.  The women began selecting their choices from the brightly colored eyeshadow, lipstick and nail polish.  That day our Ugandan version of a cosmetic counter, (the likes of which would never grace the floors of Sak's or Neiman's), painted, polished and glossed hundreds of delighted women.  I was blessed to apply eyeshadow to eyelids and polish to mud-crusted, calloused feet; bright blue seemed to be a favorite choice for both shadow and polish.

    A beautiful woman who appeared to be in her fifties approached me with a broad smile and gingerly sat down upon the tiny stool which served as our make-up chair.  She selected her choice of shadow, of course bright blue, and closed her eye. I say eye because she only had one. The lid was permanently sealed over the empty socket of the other. As I gently applied the shadow with a Q-tip, I began to imagine what her story might have been. No matter what happened to her before today, she now sat before me, smiling and enjoying just a few brief moments of pampering, a universal girl-language.

Christine told me later that day that one of the women told her she knew her husband would be mad at her for getting all painted up, but she didn't care, she knew that **that** woman loved her. I did indeed love these beautiful women. No successful major event I had conducted in any high-end department store could even come close to bringing me the joy and fulfillment I felt that day

The huge suitcase filled with medical supplies, the third purpose for my presence there, was put to use that same day.

While Christine and I were playing make-up with the women, Alan and Brent were putting to use the contents of the other suitcase I had brought with me, the medical supplies. Alan used one of the elastic braces to replace the twigs and twine that had been used to stabilize the broken arm of a little girl who had fallen from a tree a week before. The wound-care packages provided soothing relief to a man with an open wound which had afflicted him for months.

Soon it was time for the feast. Early that morning I had been privileged to accompany Christine and one of the teachers on the trip to a village on the shore of Lake Victoria to pick up the meat for the feast. To my surprise, when we made our way through the tiny ramshackle wooded structures which comprised the "shopping district", we stopped in front of the "butcher shop".

There before me, hung slabs of freshly cut carcasses surrounded by several men wearing blood stained shirts, who were busily swatting at flies in between chopping away huge chunks of meat lying before them on planks of rough wood. Christine exchanged pleasantries with them and explained to me that they were just now in the process of finishing our order. When they were done, they placed the meat inside of burlap bags handed them to the teacher who carried them and placed them in the back of our vehicle, and we were off, cargo in hand, on the hour-long trek back to the school. No refrigerated container, no thermal bag, no ice chest, just freshly slaughtered cow in burlap bags, for an hour-long journey in the hot sun of Africa.

My fear for health risk was alleviated as I observed the women preparing the food for the feast. The beef was cut into tiny one-inch squares and placed into two huge cast iron kettles filled with fiercely boiling water that sat on raging open wood-fires in the "kitchen", which was more like a shed outside of one of the school buildings. The meat sat boiling alongside two other kettles which were used to cook the rice and beans we had purchase the day before.

Only two-thirds of the beef was used to feed the 400 hungry children that day, the remaining third was used later that evening back at Makindu where the same menu was prepared to feed 200 thankful teenagers. At each banquet, I observed the same scenario, lines of hungry children, cup and bowl in hand, anxious and grateful to receive a small bit of meat, a spoonful of beans, cup of rice and a few ounces of mango juice.

As I watched the multitude of smiling faces that day, I remembered the words I had heard, standing in Neiman's,

"What are you doing when there are people starving?"

Starving does not just apply to food. There are hurting people everywhere who are hungry for even a tiny morsel of love and affection, and basic medical attention, just a touch of the hem of the Master's garment.

It was not until the last day of my time there that God revealed to me the fourth reason I had been called to these remote villages.

Brent and Alan left on an early morning flight back to the U.S. My flight was scheduled for later that evening, afforded the opportunity to speak to Deo about all of the projects he had proposed to us during our visit-- programs to develop the clinic, ways to provide much-needed income for the teachers who most of the time received no pay yet continued to educate and bring Jesus to the students. I began to write down all that he was saying, often interrupting to ask questions about the details, such as, how many bricks and jerry cans of water the women and children carried hand over hand up the hill to build the clinic. He thought that I was asking these questions to see how he had spent the money donated to build it. He misunderstood my motives and began to show me his account books to prove he had been a good steward. I closed the book and assured him that I was more than confident that he had used the money wisely. I then went on to explain that what I needed to know was the story, the story of the sacrifice and dedication of the people. It would be that story which would touch the hearts of people who might donate to his ministry.

My marketing juices had begun to flow. My mind became filled with all sorts of ways to present these programs and raise support for the ministry. I could do this. I had been trained to do this; I had successfully developed many programs for major corporations and non-profits by doing just this, researching, planning and producing ways to promote their business.

Now I knew the full reason why God had brought me there. It was all of it: the personal trials and tragedies and testimony of God's redeeming grace defeating all of the snakes which had popped up in my life; the successful careers in the world and all of the training those careers provided me. All of it was why I was here; it was to be about **His** business, bringing souls to Him.

I returned to Odessa and immediately began to prepare a prospectus detailing the programs and needs of the two schools. One of the projects Deo had proposed was what he called the Boda Boda program. Boda Boda is the name given to the motorbikes which are the primary mode of transportation in Uganda. It was his vision that if each of his teachers were to be blessed with one of these bikes, not only would it ease their sometimes 6- mile round-trip walk to the school, but also, while they were teaching, they would have the opportunity to rent out their bike to other villagers who needed to travel the sixty miles to the nearest city, thus providing an income.

In the years since my trip to Uganda, fifteen Boda Bodas have been purchased with funds donated by people who read of this need through the document conceived that day in Deo's living room. God was on the move, this time riding on Boda Boda's.

What Satan had intended for evil, my ungodly pursuit of the corporate world, God was using for good, just as He had instructed Moses to do in the wilderness when he commanded him to make a fiery serpent, place it on a staff and raise it up so that all who had been bitten by the poisonous snakes and then looked upon the raised serpent, would be healed.

If I had been given the Desire of My Heart, my granddaughter living with me, I would have been so consumed with tending to her and all of the details of her life that I would not have been available to go where God desired for me to go, to tend to the urgent needs of six-hundred children. It was difficult to let go and let God, but He had a plan. Just as I had to walk out my own place in His Kingdom, I had to release my granddaughter to discover hers.

God was now encouraging me to lift up the story of how Satan had tried to rob me of my health, my family and my very life, the story of how He had miraculously reached down and pulled me out of deaths' grip to point others to Jesus and His gift of salvation just as He had asked Moses to raise the serpent on his staff.

# CHAPTER 11

## JESUS THE ANTIVENOM

> Exodus 4:4-5 NIV
>
> Then the Lord said to him, "Reach out your hand and take it by the tail." So Moses reached out and took hold of the snake and it turned back into a staff in his hand. "This," said the Lord, "is so that they may believe that the Lord, the God of their fathers—the God of Abraham, the God of Isaac and the God of Jacob—has appeared to you.

AFTER AFRICA, I fell into a period of waiting. I knew that God had asked me to write a book about all He had done in my life, so I began spending long hours in front of my computer. But there still seemed to be more that I was to do that possibly there would be more to my story. It was not long before I received His next assignment.

Kent and I had felt led to leave our home church and search for what, we didn't exactly know. We only knew that our time there had come to an end. Our little home adjacent to the church had not only served as a meeting site where small groups grew into large groups but also as a place-- just as I had promised God that day holding onto the beams-- where anyone who needed a place to stay could find welcome. The new music minister of the church, who lived in Lubbock, would come to Odessa on the weekends. She, her husband, daughter, and baby boy began staying at our home the week after we moved in. For over three months our home became their home every weekend. A young man who was recovering from a life of drugs and tragedy stayed with us occasionally until he entered the Teen Challenge Program. Then there were the occasional friends who needed a place to stay for a time not to mention countless slumber parties hosted for our granddaughters and their friends. Our home was always open to anyone who needed a place to stay. We had lived up to our promise.

We continued in our period of waiting. It was shortly after our first year in this new home that we were called to leave our home-church to attend a new church plant that was holding services in a local junior high auditorium. We felt as if God had something in store for us, what, we were unsure of. The pastor of our new church had coincidentally begun a sermon series titled, "A Period of Waiting." Renee had begun attending services with us. She had continued on running the shelter program and had become the Center's assistant director. After leaving that position, she assisted with the start-up of a new shelter program in Midland. Now she too felt that she was awaiting God's direction for the next season of her life. We didn't have to wait long.

On a cold December morning in 2014, I was awakened by the Holy Spirit for another of those 3 AM talks with Daddy, (*what I affectionately call my Father God*). I had learned early on that when this happened, I had better get up, grab a pen and paper, and record the message. Failure to do so would most often result in me trying to remember His words and being frustrated that I could not remember something important. On this particular morning I received a series of clear, concise instructions which began with these words,

"It is to be called The Well."

In rapid succession I was told that I was not to run The Well, only to get it started. I was not to take government funding because Jesus would be Lord of it. We had experienced what it was like to be forbidden to even mention the name of Jesus at Angel House due to the precise guidelines set out for government grant recipients. Admittedly we did not adhere to this policy for at Angel House, Jesus was the topic of most conversations. He was not only discussed He was praised, thanked and worshipped. We saw our residents turn from witchcraft and other such satanic persuasions through the His saving Grace.

His explicit words to me were that He would provide the funding. I was cautioned not to proceed like I had done with Angel House, running around trying to do it on my own. He would provide a place and the means. I was told it would not be a place just for women who had suffered abuse but also for women seeking God, a place where they could dance in the Lord and create Spirit-inspired art. He then told me to get busy, that I had a deadline.

Kent had become used to my early morning meetings with God. He would always ask me if everything was OK, the memory of the times when I had become ill in the night still an ever present fear. This particular morning, when he asked and I began to relay to him all of the instructions I had been given, he sat straight up in bed and said, "There will be no shelter!"

His concern was understandably founded in the memory of how the last shelter program had impacted our lives. I was quick to reassure him that my instructions had been clear: I was not to run the well, only give birth to it.

I prayed about this message for several days before I called Renee. As I relayed all of the information the God had given me, she replied in her low even tone, "Of course He did!" We both committed to pray about it for the next few months. In February, Renee and I, Evelyn, a close friend who had come alongside us at Angel House, plus one of their friends, Sega, gathered around Renee's kitchen table and formed the beginning board of The Well Hand of Grace. Hand of Grace had been added by Renee from a vision God had given her which showed the hand of God with each of His five fingers representing the five programs of The Well.

I began writing the 501C3 application, and sometime in March, I submitted it. Thinking that it would take three-to-six months for approval, we scheduled a community forum to announce the creation of The Well Hand of Grace for June 11.

In my eagerness to bring this project to fruition, I ignored one of the basic instructions I had been given by God and began scouring the city for a possible location.  The Holy Spirit was quick to bring me back in line.  As I was sitting in the parking lot of a vacant building which was for sale, cell phone in hand leaving a message for my realtor, I began to replay the words spoken to me early that morning in December, "Don't do it like you did last time.  I will provide the place."  I quickly hung up the phone and resting my head on the steering wheel, asked God to forgive me.

It was now May, the camp season was just around the corner, and Kent and I were preparing once again to trek up the mountain.  Kent, as usual, had reserved two weeks of his vacation for camp, a ritual he had performed for almost thirty years.

On our last visit to the camp in January, Bev and Rusty, the couple who had run the camp for forty years, had told us that they planned to retire soon.  They asked us if we wanted to take over running the camp when they stepped down.

We left the mountain that day in a state of shock.  Could what we envisioned for our retirement years be actually coming true?  For the next four months, we weighed the pros and cons of this proposition.  We were not sure just how soon the opportunity might present itself.  Kent would be eligible in March for early retirement from his company of almost thirty-six years.  We had felt that we were in a period of waiting for several months now. Could this possibly be God's plan for our lives?

It was now May and as Kent slipped into Summer-camp-mode he became focused on what he would be responsible for this year.  Although we no longer attended the same church where he had worked with the youth director, we had kept in close contact with him, and Kent was now serving as his assistant and as usual, "Dorm Dad". He was in his element.

Kent had taken his children to this camp since they were little. While there, our daughter (Kent's by birth) had felt God's call to attend Dallas Christian College as she became acquainted with the various camp teams from DCC. She had met her husband at the college, and now as graduates, they and our precious third granddaughter, served as the resident directors in the men's dorm. They had made us aware that there would soon be a vacancy in the resident director's position in the women's dorm. This information had from time to time entered our conversations as a "what-if."

When camp week was over, on the trip down the mountain we received a fateful phone call from our daughter at the college. The women's resident director had resigned that morning. The position was open. We made a phone call and set up a Skype interview for the following week, at their request, June 11, the same day of The Well forum.

The forum location, of course, had been provided by God's hand. Russ, a DCC graduate and the pastor of Asbury United Methodist Church where Renee had attended conferences, gladly offered the use of his banquet hall. The Well Hand of Grace was received with a resounding yes from those gathered. When the meeting concluded, Pastor Russ asked the four of us to follow him into an office adjacent to the banquet hall. There he presented to us the office we where we now stood, as the new home of The Well Hand of Grace.

He explained that we would also be provided with a phone and have access to the entire church facility. God had shown up in a great and powerful way. His promises are true, He did provide.

Immediately after the forum, Kent and I had to hurry home for the Skype interview with the college, which was scheduled to begin exactly one hour after the forum ended. God had said that I had a timeline, and I did. He had planned His schedule down to the very hour.

This was the first job interview I had ever conducted barefooted. This was the first job interview Kent had ever experienced (previously he had only ever been required to fill out an application.) Through the course of the interview, we were asked a variety of questions, like how we were with cultural diversity. We chuckled at that one. As Kent likes to put it, "I don't see color." As Renee, Pepper or should I say Ebony (we have changed from Salt and Pepper to Ebony and Ivory cause now we are more elegant) puts it, "You are the blackest girl I know!"

Another of the questions brought a smile and possibly a look of puzzlement to our faces. We were asked how we might handle being wakened in the middle of the night by a student with a problem. The interviewer went on to explain that you never knew what situation you might face when you opened the door. No sooner had he uttered those words than he realized to whom he was asking this question.

The Crisis Center and Kent's position with his company had required that we both carry pagers and be available to respond to a crisis at any time. He had been accustomed to his company pager going off or receiving an emergency phone call from the answering service in the middle of the night. Kent had also served as a crisis-volunteer at the center. Together we had seen and responded to just about everything. The interview concluded with the information that they were considering one other couple for the position. They promised to get back in touch with us the following week which was the second week of camp.

That particular week, two camp-teamers from DCC stayed with us the night before camp to break up the journey from Dallas to New Mexico. We had often times invited various camp teams and youth groups to stay at our home when needed. Now we had the opportunity to serve both DCC and the camp.

The week was filled with the usual activities. Kent and I spent time with Bev and Rusty in further discussion about the possibility of our taking over the camp. During this conversation we told them about our interview with the college the week before. They assured us that God would reveal where He desired to plant us.

On Thursday, Kent and I decided to forgo the customary hike up the mountain to view the top ridge to McKittrick Canyon; it had been a long week, and we needed a rest. As we were drifting off to sleep, Kent's cell phone rang. It was the dean of students from DCC. one of the men who had conducted our Skype interview. He opened with, "We have decided to hire the other couple who applied for the position." Immediately Kent and I looked at each other and smiled. We felt that God had just given us the answer to where He desired for us to be--we were to take over the camp.

The next phrase we heard was, "However, we would like to propose to you a different position, a volunteer position, something totally unique." He went on to say that after the cabinet had reviewed our résumés and based on our interview, wanted to create two new positions for us. He then laughed as he added, "You wouldn't want to live in two dorm rooms as volunteers would you?"

Again we looked at each other and without hesitation said, "Yes."

It took a few moments for our answer to sink into our caller. He then began to outline the vision the cabinet had for us. They were primarily interested in Kent's ability to serve as coordinator of the mentoring program and eventually train to possibly serve as a campus chaplain. He proposed that I might assist with the marketing of the college or "something".

The dean then asked us when we felt we might be available to move to Dallas. Immediately Kent's knack for planning kicked in. He explained that we would have to first sell our home and that it would take 60 days from the time he gave notice to his company until the completion of his retirement process but most importantly, we would have to sell our house. Kent then asked, "So should we go ahead and sell our house?" The response was immediate, "Sell your house."

On Saturday, we and the two camp teamers left for Odessa. We told the two about our new position on their campus, and they were ecstatic.

On Sunday, Kent had to go back to work and I began to awaken the students from DCC who had once again spent the night with us. As I prepared to take our guests to church, I had an idea. Actually, I believe that the Holy Spirit prompted me to call the man who had built our home. I called and left a message for him and followed up with a text. I explained what Kent and I planned to undertake and asked if he would be interested in buying-back our house. He immediately texted back, "Let's talk. I'll be back in town on Tuesday morning." God was working.

That Monday, as Kent and I were standing in line at the grocery store, our builder called. He said that he needed to go out of town again and could we talk about the sale now. I asked Kent. He nodded his head, and I resumed the conversation. He asked how much we wanted for the house. I conferred again with Kent and repeated the figure we had agreed on. The next words I heard were, "I'll have a check ready for pick-up this week." He had agreed to pay us $10,000 more for the house than we had paid for it just two and a half years before.

In the parking lot of the grocery store, Kent and I sat inside our pick-up for what seemed like hours just staring at each other. The past five days had brought us from living securely in our new home with Kent entrenched in a six-figure-plus position with a company he had been with for thirty-six years, to now about to sell our home, leave a comfortable lifestyle, and embark upon an unknown future with no paycheck, and live in 385 square feet in a college dorm. What were we thinking?

In 2013 I had read the tiny book *Radical*, by David Platt. Its cover was blank except for a tiny upside down drawing of a church building. The book is filled with stories of people who had turned their lives upside down for Christ, people who had sold everything, walked away from lucrative careers, to follow in the footsteps of the Fisherman. This book changed me. I had asked myself, would I be willing to walk away from all I knew, friends, family, career to follow Jesus? I had experienced starting over so many times already in my life (I had moved thirty-six times, to be precise). I had been alone without a home and nowhere to go, the memory of which was still fresh in my mind.

But would Kent be willing to shuck it all, our home, his secure position, our friends? I never asked him. I knew that a big portion of who he believed himself to be was wrapped up in the stability of his job. Thank God that it was, for if he had not been so stable and dependable, we would not have been in the secure financial position we were now. Had it not been for the wonderful insurance provided by his company, Oxy USA, we would be paying off my astronomical medical bills for the next hundred years.

I remember the day when I called to tell my father that Kent and I planned to be married. He had never met Kent, and here his daughter was, a thousand miles away, about to step off into matrimony yet again. He was all too aware of how the last two disastrous marital unions had turned out for me. He had been instrumental in helping me pick up the pieces of my life each time. The only question he asked me when I told him about Kent was, "How long has he worked for his company?"

My father was a long-term employee himself, only working for two companies his entire life. Stability was also part of who he was. When I told him that Kent had been employed at the same company for nineteen years, it was all he needed to know. He believed that you could tell a lot about a man by this one simple fact, it showed stability (God only knew I had never experienced that in my adult life.)

That says it all. God knew. God knew from the beginning who I was and who Kent was. He knew our hearts. This is what He meant when He spoke to me those two times when I lay flat out in surrender beside my bed.

"This is **My** marriage and I do not want it to end!"

This is what He had planned for us from the beginning. He knew that when the call came, we would both be ready to say, yes Lord, send me. We had become "radical."

Kent finally broke the silence in the truck outside the grocery store and said, "Let's call the school and tell them that we are on our way."

We called the dean of students on the speakerphone of the truck. When we told him that we had just sold our home, there was silence on the other end. In shock, he said, "But I just told you to sell it last Thursday!"

Jokingly, we told him that we were sorry that it had taken so long and that we usually worked faster than this. Our God can accomplish great things in the blink of an eye. Actually three days is a pretty long time when you consider that He created the entire universe in only six.

Then the Holy Spirit prompted me to ask a question I had never imagined asking, "What do you do at the school for sexual assault and domestic violence education?" His tone suddenly became very serious and he asked why I was asking that question. When I explained that part of what I had done in my career with the Crisis Center was to teach courses on these matters in the community and school district, he immediately asked how soon I would be able to move to Dallas. He went on to tell us that due to Title IX and the Clery Act and the requirement of all institutions of higher education to comply with the prevention and education of both issues, it was the number one priority of the campus and that there was a fast-approaching deadline for compliance with hefty fines for failure to do so.

The struggles and heartache I had endured at the Crisis Center, all of the training I had received would now be used at the college to help future ministers and missionaries prepare for their calling, God's Business.

Kent explained that he could submit his application for retirement immediately but would be required to remain in Odessa working for the next sixty-days, however, I could move immediately.

So two weeks later, after packing up the things we would be able to take with us, giving away or selling the rest, I loaded up our pick-up with a few of my belongings and moved to Dallas to begin doing what God had prepared me to do. Kent's work schedule at the time was a week on and a week off, so on his weeks off, he would fly to Dallas and begin doing what God had prepared him to do through almost thirty years of working with youth groups, minister to, as he liked to call them, "his kids".

During this transition period, Kent was taking care of the myriad details involved with his retirement process. With no income but my meager $1,100 dollars a month from Social Security, our budget was going to be tight. Kent would not be eligible to tap into his 401K for 4 and a half years. Although we did have money in the bank from the sale of our home and the previous house, we did not intend to deplete this nest egg.

During one of the many phone calls to his human-resources advocate, God provided the proof that we were indeed following His direction and not our own. The advocate had discovered that because Kent had originally been employed by a separate company which, several years after his employment date, had been purchased by Oxy USA, the company he now worked for, the retirement fund he had begun on the date of his original employment till then, had been placed in a, "bubble", a separate fund from his 401K and had been gaining interest all of these years. She then went on to advise him that he could begin receiving funds from that account immediately. We had been obedient, taken a leap of faith and God had provided.

I remember the word which God had spoken to me that day just a few years ago: "But if you had the desires of your heart, you wouldn't be available for what I need you to do." If we had still been busy caring for a teenager, working to help her complete her education, there is no way we would have been available or even able to pack up and move to Dallas to live in two dorm rooms. There was that word, "available". He needed for me to be available to follow His leading.

My heart still aches for the time I missed with her. It aches for all of the time lost with both of my granddaughters, but God has called me to minister to a whole campus full of young men and women who need to be shown His love. Instead of one teenager to love and care for, I live with sometimes forty young women and together with the young men in the boy's dorm and the off-campus students, counsel them as they are seeking God's direction for their lives, preparing to serve Him in either full-time ministry or to be his disciples in the workplace.

"Phat Daddy" and "Mama Sue" came to Dallas Christian College with résumés only God could have orchestrated. I am not talking only about our professional careers, even though the experience and knowledge we gleaned from those positions have certainly been used at the college. I am talking about the life lessons we learned, both separately and together, those things learned by living both with God and away from God. It was my times away from walking with Him that have provided the greatest impact on the students I counsel. There has been not one single issue which a student has come to me with that I have not either encountered personally or have dealt with in some capacity at the Crisis Center or the business world.

I do not wear my testimony as a badge of honor, nor do I try to conceal it in shame. It is there to show that God never left me, no matter how far I had fallen away from His path. I was the one who walked, even ran, away from Him. No matter how far I had fallen, God was just a thought, a prayer, just a breath away.

My great-great-great aunt, who spent countless hours toiling in the fields, plowing, and planting, had no way of knowing that her actions would mean something to me so many years later. She had learned to be constantly on her guard, never knowing when a snake might appear. My grandmother, Ma, couldn't have known that the words she spoke, "Just killin' snakes," would one day be my battle cry.

I'm sure that occasionally my great-great aunt was bitten by one of those snakes she grabbed; it was an occupational hazard. I am also sure that she knew which snakes were poisonous and which ones weren't. With people, sometimes it is too difficult tell just who you are dealing with, where they are coming from. That is when you must rely on the discernment God provides through the Holy Spirit. On those occasions, when I know that I sense that something I have encountered is not from God but from the serpent, I know that I must stop and address it with prayer at the very moment of encounter, preventing it from slithering into my life. Killin' snakes is in my bloodline. Killing **The** snake is now my legacy.

Because of my research for this book, and the newfound interest in my family history, I was about to reveal yet another legacy. I had always suspected that my family was of Jewish ancestry, but not on Ma's side, my paternal grandfather's side.

Two years ago I had my DNA tested, and my suspicions were confirmed. I discovered that I am descended from Sub Saharan Africa and also the

Ashkenazi Jewish bloodline from Germany. My middle name, Suzanne, was given to me because my earthly father desired for me to have his father's initials. It was important to him. Names are important to Our Heavenly Father too.

Suzanne in Hebrew is Shoshanna, which means, "Lily." In Luke 8:1-3 NRSV you will read,

"Soon afterwards he went on through cities and villages, proclaiming and bringing the good news of the kingdom of God. The twelve were with him, as well as some women who had been cured of evil spirits and infirmities: Mary, called Magdalene, from whom seven demons had gone out, and Joanna, the wife of Herod's steward Chuza, and Susanna, and many others, who provided for them out of their resources.

Women, delivered of demons and illness, working with Jesus and the disciples in **His** Father's business.

In my research, I found reference to a story entitled, "Susanna and the Elders", it is included in the Book of Daniel (as chapter 13) by the Roman Catholic and Eastern Orthodox churches. It is one of the additions to Daniel, considered apocryphal by Protestants. As the story goes, Susanna was falsely accused by lecherous voyeurs. They accosted her, threatening to claim that she was meeting a young man in the garden unless she agrees to have sex with them. She refuses to be blackmailed and is arrested and about to be put to death for promiscuity when the young Daniel came to her rescue and managed to prove that the men were lying. The parallels between a few of the details of these stories of two Biblical Susanna's and my life were not lost on me: my career at the Rape Crisis Center,

Angel House, and the ministry that Kent and I share as volunteers at the college.

When I was in Israel I was blessed by several encounters with that name, Shoshanna, encounters that confirmed to me that God's hand had been on my life from its beginning and in so many ways.

I had always felt some unexplained connection to the Jewish people, which was the reason why in college I wrote a research paper on the Holocaust. I remain to this day haunted by the knowledge of the atrocities inflicted upon God's chosen people. As I read the Old Testament I am constantly aware of the struggles they have endured throughout history.

After completing the tour of the main building of the Holocaust Memorial, Yad Vashem, in Jerusalem, I walked down the path to the Children's Memorial. As I took my first step into the darkness of the room, surrounded by the twinkling points of light, each one representing a child that was killed, I heard these words, "And Shoshanna, from Germany." That occurrence in and of itself is not unusual; the names of each of the 1.5 million children are repeated continuously while the memorial is open. But the fact that my name, Shoshanna, would be spoken just as I entered, and it was precisely, Shoshanna from Germany--that was my confirmation that God had called me, His daughter, by name to be exactly who I am for his purposes, to take on His mission to spread the news of His Redeeming-Grace to as many souls as I can with my testimony.

The words of Isaiah 43: 1-7 NIV, say it far better than anything I have written on the pages of this book:

" But now, this is what the Lord says he who created you, Jacob, he who formed you, Israel: Do not fear, for I have redeemed you; I have summoned you by name; you are mine. When you pass through the waters, I will be with you; and when you pass through the rivers, they will not sweep over you. When you walk through the fire, you will not be burned; the flames will not set you ablaze. For I am the Lord your God, the Holy One of Israel, your Savior."

He has called me by name, just as He is calling all of His children to return to Him, to teach them that when Satan turns up in their lives, they have the power through Him to reach down, grab the serpent by the tail, and fling it out of their lives through faith in Jesus.

Some snake handlers like the man I observed that day at the rattlesnake roundup, gradually build up an immunity to venom each time they are bitten. Snake charmers have been known to drink small quantities of watered-down snake venom in order to protect themselves from their deadly business partner's occasional strikes. Unfortunately, none of us will ever be immune to Satan's appearance in our lives. He is only one little white lie, one harmless movie, one flashy magazine away from slithering his way into our minds, but we have the most powerful antivenom in the world, the power of Jesus Christ. He drank the poison for us. He suffered the excruciating effects of Satan's strongest venom full-strength on the cross. When he arose just three days later, He proved that He was more powerful than anything Satan could throw at Him.

He is waiting to forgive us when we allow ourselves to become snared by the evil of this world. Forgiveness is what it's all about. Forgiveness heals not only the person who is forgiven but the person who forgives.

In 2017 my first husband passed away. I had forgiven him for the many troubles he had caused in my life a long time ago. When my daughter, called to tell me that he had suffered a stroke and was not expected to live much longer, my heart sank. I immediately rounded up my prayer warriors in three states to begin praying for him. We prayed that he had made things right with God. We prayed that he would go to heaven. How ironic. I remembered the time when I had said, "It isn't fair. All he had to do was say he was sorry and ask God to be forgiven and he would get to go to heaven!" I wished evil upon him, but forgiveness had changed all of that. I was never able to tell him that I had forgiven him. I should have made the effort.

When I relayed this message to my prayer partners, the response I received was unexpected. Many of them had known my story-my history with this man. I received messages that said that they too were in the midst of dealing with forgiveness and needed to hear my words. Each one of us has that power to forgive and be forgiven available to us right now. The power to be free from the clutches of un-forgiveness that can open you up to the attacks of the enemy.

As I look back at my life, I have been drawn to the story of Job. I wrote a sermon based on my life entitled "Job's Daughter." I had always heard the phrase, the patience of Job. As I studied the scripture. I realized that Job was not patient. He cried out many times to God with questions about why his life had been plagued with destruction, loss of loved ones, and disease. I found it disturbing that God would have allowed, even directed. Satan to focus his attention on Job. I had felt much as Job had so many times when I felt the effects of Satan's presence in my life and that God was somehow responsible for all of the chaos. Then I read this particular passage:

Job 36: 5-11 NIV

"God is mighty, but despises no one; He is mighty, and firm in his purpose. "He does not keep the wicked alive but gives the afflicted their rights. He does not take his eyes off the righteous; he enthrones them with kings and exalts them forever. But if people are bound in chains, held fast by cords of affliction, He tells them what they have done—that they have sinned arrogantly. He makes them listen to correction and commands them to repent of their evil. If they obey and serve him, they will spend the rest of their days in prosperity and their years in contentment."

I was afflicted, bound by the chords of sin, the chains of guilt and shame, Satan's most powerful venom. God reached down and grabbed hold of me in between life and death, and forced me to listen to His correction. Then He gave me the command to join Him in, "Cleaning up this earth."

In Genesis fifty you will find the story of Joseph a young man who was betrayed by his brothers and sold into slavery. His story is one of how, with God's help, he survived very difficult circumstances to emerge strong and successful. When he had the opportunity to face the brothers who had betrayed him, he spoke these words, Genesis 50: 20 NIV "You intended to harm me, but God intended it for good to accomplish what is now being done, the saving of many lives."

Satan the snake intended for all of the disaster, disease and heartbreak to destroy me. Joseph forgave his brothers, so must we.

It is my prayer my mission that through my testimony, this story, that someone will see themselves and realize that God can deliver them just as He has delivered me.

In the twenty first book of Numbers, verse six, it says that God did send the venomous snakes among the disobedient children of Israel and they bit them and many died. They asked Moses to pray to God to take the snakes away. When Moses prayed God told him to place the snake upon the stick and that all who looked upon it would live. Not only did God take away the snakes, He provided a way for those who had been bitten by them to live. That is what He has done for me and for you by sending Jesus to take the fall, for our fall away from Him. He is the cure and the protection from being bitten again by the sharp teeth of Satan.

All Kent and I own in the world is what is inside the walls of our two tiny dorm rooms, two storage closets plus our faithful pick-up, yet I believe that I am the wealthiest woman on earth. I have Jesus living inside of me. I know without a shadow of a doubt that my life has a purpose. He loves me and has a plan for my life. He has always had a plan for my life. I was saved from Satan's clutches to show the world that there is no circumstance you may find yourself in, no darkness so severe, no affliction so crippling, nothing, nothing, that can separate you from the love of God.

As Kent and I cultivate the fields of the college, the memory of our struggles is never far away from our thoughts.  Occasionally Satan's ploys still pop up in our lives, but the lessons we have learned through our nineteen years of marriage have served not only us but the students and families we minister to as well.  We know that we are here to be examples of what God desires a marriage to be.  We are open and honest about our failures, the times we gave control to Satan, right along with our triumphs.  We are here to witness to young men and women who desire to become ministers, missionaries, worship leaders, teachers, psychiatrists, educators, and business leaders that it is important whom you choose to be your partner in ministry and in life.  We are not perfect, not by a long shot, but we are perfect in God's eyes.

Each of us has a purpose for being on this earth, and it is God's purpose.  Just as Job found it hard to understand why he was allowed to endure all of the tragic events in his life, Kent and I understand that each event in ours has served to make us who we are and that God has rewarded us for remaining true to Him.

Job 42:12 NIV, "The Lord blessed the latter part of Job's life more than the former part.....

God was faithful to Job for his persistence and he rewarded him.  It is now, now that we are living within the will of God, we are blessed beyond measure, and our latter days are certainly greater than our former.  It is the memory of those times when Kent would come home, roll back the carpet and hold me as we danced, that inspired us to place these words by Viviane Greene on the door of our bedroom,

*"Life isn't about waiting for the storm to pass...It's about learning to Dance in the Rain."*

If you have read the entire Bible, you know how the whole story ends. The battle at Armageddon is won by the only one who has the power to defeat Satan, the God of all creation. He will crush the head of the serpent once and for all.

You have the power to make your later days greater than the first part of your life through accepting the freedom from Satan's power, which is freely provided through the gift of His Son Jesus Christ. You don't have to start a shelter, sell your home and turn your life upside down or donate thousands of dollars to charities to receive this freedom-it is freely given.

It is not lost on me that the church and tiny school I attended were named St. Paul's, and that the confirmation verse I was given was Ephesians 2:8-9, "For by grace are ye saved through faith; and that not of yourselves: it is the gift of God: Not of works, lest any man should boast."

In Jerusalem, I found myself standing in a room beneath the house of Caiaphas, the man who had been the president of the Sanhedrin council. Caiaphas had convinced Pontius Pilate that Jesus was a threat to the Roman Empire and should be executed. Our tour guide explained to us that this tiny stone carved room could possibly be where Jesus was held during His trial. As we looked at the hollowed out openings in the stone beam above our heads she described the process of how the holes were used to secure the prisoner's hands with ropes while they were beaten and or flogged.

It hit me in a wave of grief I had never experienced before. The image of Jesus hands being tied with ropes while he was being beaten was too much for me to bear. My thoughts returned to the operating room and the moment I had become acutely aware of the great suffering Jesus endured during His trial and crucifixion; the time when I realized just how much He loved me and how much His Father God loved me.

I felt as if I couldn't breathe. I ran back up the narrow stairs leading from the cell, out into the freedom of daylight. I found a seat inside the adjacent chapel and slumped over sobbing into my hands; warm tears of grief intermingled with joy streaming down my face. I was overcome with the extreme gravity of just what my sin had cost. I was embraced with the joy that I was no longer required to pay the price for those sins.

. It was not anything I had done in my life that saved me and gave me freedom. It was purely by God's Grace.

I am not alone in this. Jesus has done the only great thing necessary for you to also receive freedom. He died on the cross to allow you the opportunity to accept His power to rescue you and to change your life. Through The Holy Spirit, He will speak to you, just as He has spoken to me all of my life, I just had not been still enough to listen. It had been His voice that I had heard urging me on when life was painful; His voice warning me of danger or wrong turns; His voice whispering tender words of love and healing to my broken heart.

In Matthew 10:27 NIV, it says, "What I tell you in the dark, speak in the daylight; what is whispered in your ear, proclaim from the roofs."

He spoke to me, I heard His voice and now I will not be silent. If He asks me to, I will climb up to the rooftop and sing His praises. He saved me from a life of sickness and shame. He saved my life from physical death but more importantly eternal death.

Be still, listen. The voice you might be hearing is saying, "This is for you. I am the voice you hear in your head right now. It is me. You too can be free. Accept Jesus Christ into your life, today, this moment as your Lord and Savior and you will be truly free."

Contact Information:

www.suearrington.com

suearrington88@gmail.com